THE GOD WHO GRIEVES

BISHOP F. JOSEPHUS (JOEY) JOHNSON, II

xulon PRESS

The God Who Grieves
by Bishop F. Josephus (Joey) Johnson, II

Printed in the United States of America.

ISBN 9781498484251

www.xulonpress.com

Special thanks to Delores Jones
for her ongoing literary help.

PREFACE

This is a series of messages that I preached at the end of 2012. These messages entertain God's grief, as it is related to us in His Word. I have chosen to keep the same format and context as the series, i.e. with some corrections and minor additions.

Some of the illustrations and news references are dated, but the truths that are being presented are timeless.

Even though I have written a number of books, my strength is public speaking. So, these are the enhanced manuscripts that I used for my sermons.

A manuscript is different than a book. A manuscript is written to be spoken, so I pray that you will be able to use your imagination to imagine sitting in my church and prayerfully listening to the sermon.

I pray that the Spirit will use these manuscripts to change your view of God, the Father, so that, so that you might come into more intimate fellowship with Him. I believe that will happen as you begin to see His grief, compassion, and love for His people, which includes me and you.

Be blessed!

Bishop F. Josephus Johnson, II
Presiding Prelate of the Beth-El Fellowship of Visionary Churches
Senior Pastor of The House of the Lord

SERMON #1

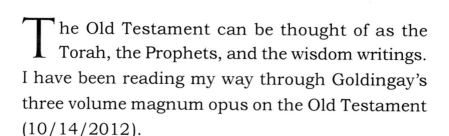

The Old Testament can be thought of as the Torah, the Prophets, and the wisdom writings. I have been reading my way through Goldingay's three volume magnum opus on the Old Testament (10/14/2012).

In the process, I also read two books by German theologian, Walter Brueggemann: *The Prophetic Imagination* and *The Practice of Prophetic Imagination*. In both of these books, Brueggemann works with the following thesis:

> "Prophetic preaching is an effort to imagine the world as though YHWH, the creator of heaven and earth, the Father of our Lord Jesus Christ whom we Christians name as Father, Son,

and Spirit, is a real character and a defining agent in the world."[1]

Brueggemann's thesis comes from his study of the Old Testament prophets. Old Testament prophets were **not** simply predictors or social activists, but rather divine spokespersons of YHWH, who—in the light of YHWY's narrative—imagined the world as though YHWH was a real character and a defining agent in the world.

You are probably thinking, "Don't all Saints see YHWH as a real character and a defining agent in the world?" Well, quite frankly, "No!" Our modern conceptions and perceptions of God are all over the place, but mostly we see God as more of an idea than a real being! **God is more of a construct of our imagination than a real, relational being!**

Particularly, because God is invisible, I believe many people don't actually imagine the world as though YHWH is a real character, i.e. real like anybody that you can see, hear, smell, and touch.

Furthermore, since I have taught in the past that many modern people are practical atheists,

---

[1] Walter Brueggemann, *The Practice of Prophetic Imagination: Preaching an Emancipating Word*, Fortress Press, Minneapolis, Minnesota, 2012, p. 23.

who act as if there is **no** God; the world is **not** imagined as though YHWH is a defining agent in the world. For the most part, He simply does **not** come to mind! Even for the religious and theological people who comprise Christianity, there are major problems in biblically conceiving and perceiving God, i.e. how we think about and sense God. The continuum ranges from those who think that God has determined everything and we have **no** choice to those who believe that God has created processes that He cannot control or alter. God's power ranges from total control, to influence, to total inability to control.

And even, in all of this, is God acting outside of history or in history?

Consequently, Brueggemann has explored the worldview of the Old Testament prophets and shares with us His summary of how they see life and operate.

Again, Brueggemann's thesis is that these OT prophets imagine the world as though YHWH, the Creator of heaven and earth, the Father of our Lord Jesus, the Christ, whom we Christians name as Father, Son, and Spirit, is a real character and a defining agent in the world.

In operating from this worldview, the Old Testament prophets often find themselves in the divide between the current dominant story of reality and God's story of reality, i.e. whatever the world believes at a given point in time and God's story that is revealed in the text of the Bible.

However, the current worldview has so inundated those of us who live in American that our cultural lenses distort God's story! Even though we believe we read the Bible and then use it as a filter to discern the world around us, the truth is that the world around us is so powerful that we read the Bible through our social and cultural lenses.

Those of us who are trying to proclaim God's story, from His Word, can learn some things from these Old Testament prophets. These Old Testament prophets often used the power of poetry to contrast God's story of reality with the dominant story of reality, whether that was the reality of Pharaoh or Nebuchadnezzar or even Solomon. **Poetry is the language of relationships. Poetry reaches past the head and stimulates the heart!**

The invisible YHWH is often treated as if He is **not** real and **not** a defining agent in the world. Yet, time and time again, we see YHWH reveal His reality in various actions, as He helps to define Israel's reality when He acts in her history. **And this action is related in poetic form.**

The problem is that the dominant culture, whether it is Israelite, Egyptian, Babylonian, Roman, or American, is <u>not</u> interested in God's story and is resistant to His prophets! Yet, the prophets come with a message of hope to people who are in <u>***unconscious***</u> denial and despair about the circumstances.

Hence the prophets deal at length with denial, despair, loss, grief, numbness, and newness. **We shall look at loss and grief as imaged and poetically stated by the prophets.**

I was deeply impacted by these two books and the way the author talked about grief. I was particularly struck by the following quote:

> "Israel of course has a long liturgical, pastoral history of grief work in its many lament Psalms. But those laments are especially mobilized around the crisis of the fall of Jerusalem, its king, its

temple, and its status as the chosen of YHWH."[2]

This quote sparked a cascade of thoughts connected to grief, grief work, grief work in the Bible, the grief process, etc., etc., etc. You all know that grief has been a very important area of my theology, ministry, work, and life. Consequently, I began to think about our grief recovery ministry, which is called "From Midnight to Dawn." This is a metaphor of the healing that takes place when a person faithfully travels the grief recovery pathway or takes the grief recovery journey.

The person who processes grief, in a healthy way, journeys from midnight to dawn...from darkness to light...from closing windows of opportunity to open doors of possibility.

The psalm that we shall return to over and over again is

Psalm 30:5 (NASB), "5 For His anger is but for a moment, His favor is for a lifetime; Weeping may last for the

---

[2] Walter Brueggemann, *The Practice of Prophetic Imagination: Preaching an Emancipating Word*, Fortress Press, Minneapolis, Minnesota, 2012, p. 74.

night, But a shout of joy *comes* in the morning."

We shall ask ourselves,

- "How long is a moment or a night?"
- "How dark and discomforting is the night?"

We shall ask these questions because one such night was the Children of Israel's long era of exile from their country.

We shall also ask ourselves,

- "What happened in the comma that separated the night from the morning?"
- "How did momentary anger become life-long favor?"
- "How did an entire night of weeping become a shout of joy in the morning?"

We shall attempt to reveal the fact that in the comma is wilderness, blockage, crucifixion, repentance, grief, struggle, failure. We shall repeatedly note the following pattern, which is seen in various life situations:

The Children of Israel traveled from

Egypt ➜ Wilderness ➜ Promised Land

The process of creativity follows the pathway of

Birth   ➜ Blockage   ➜ Breakthrough
                                      (Creativity)

The life of Jesus moves from

Birth   ➜ Crucifixion   ➜ Resurrection

Because God loves us, He allowed us choice, which led to

Sin ➜ Repentance ➜ Salvation

In fact, because of sin, arising out of The Fall of Adam and Eve, life can be looked at as a series of losses, and the pattern of loss is

Loss ➜ Grief   ➜ Possibility

In fact, superimposed over all of life, is the pattern of

Life → Struggle   → New life

I believe, and I talked about it during our last Counter-Culture Club (2012), that this pattern is so prevalent in all of reality, because this reality was created by God. Everything that God creates bears His signature or DNA. As such, this may represent some deep reality in the Godhead, which is seen in

Creation → The Fall   → The New Creation

I'm not saying that there is sin in the Godhead, because we believe the Godhead to be holy. However, this does not categorically rule out relational struggle. It might look like Jesus' discussion with the Father, while on the cross, about letting the cup of suffering pass from Him.

In fact, I began to think of a number of metaphors, because I am coming to understand more and more deeply that metaphors may be the most powerful teaching tools that God has every created. **Indeed, language itself may be nothing but metaphor!**

I began to think about grief recovery work as a passage from darkness to light, from death to life, from immaturity to maturity, from hopelessness to hope, etc.

I began to think about grief recovery work as a door to a different reality. Unless there is grief, **denial** blocks the way towards change and people become numb and stuck in their familiar pain.

I began to think about grief as an energizing process, in addition to the de-energizing that we are all familiar with. We know that grief can be emotionally draining and physically tiring. **We don't know much about grief being emotionally energizing!**

I began to consider the grief of God, which is seldom mentioned, much less talked about.

I began to see that God does grief work and His grief work is a model for us.

I began to see God's grief as a possible theodicy for God's anger and indignation. "Theodicy" is a branch of religion that defends God's goodness and justice in the face of evil (*WordWeb Pro 6.76*).

At some point, I plan do a future series, on Wednesday nights, to help us face the powerful dilemma of seeing God's goodness and justice in the face of evil, persistent evil, and/or horrendous evil (Hitler).

However, in this particular series, we shall be working on a theodicy for God's anger and righteous indignation.

I began to see the need to explore all of these possibilities more deeply.

(So, let's begin a new series: "From Midnight to Dawn: The Movement towards Morning.")

Because this is an introductory message, that's about as far as we can go today. However, for the moment, we rejoice in

> Psalm 30:5 (NASB), "⁵ For His anger is but for a moment, His favor is for a lifetime; Weeping may last for the night, But a shout of joy *comes* in the morning."

SERMON #2

We just began a new series on grief that was spawned by two books, *The Prophetic Imagination* and *The Practice of Prophetic Imagination*, by the German theologian, Walter Brueggemann

I was deeply impacted by these two books, in particular by the way the author talked about biblical grief. I was arrested by the following quote:

> "Israel of course has a long liturgical, pastoral history of grief work in its many lament Psalms. But those laments are especially mobilized around the crisis of the fall of Jerusalem, its king, its temple, and its status as the chosen of YHWH."[3]

[3] Walter Brueggemann, *The Practice of Prophetic Imagination: Preaching an Emancipating Word*, Fortress Press, Minneapolis, Minnesota, 2012, p. 74.

This quote sparked a cascade of thoughts connected to grief, grief work, grief work in the Bible, the grief process, etc., etc., etc. **You all know that grief has been a very important area of my theology, ministry, work, and life.** So, I began to think about our grief recovery ministry, which is called "From Midnight to Dawn." This is a metaphor of the healing that takes place when a person faithfully travels the grief recovery pathway or takes the grief recovery journey. **They travel from the darkness of midnight to the morning light of dawn!**

In *The Practice of Prophetic Imagination*, Brueggemann touches on the following psalm, which we shall use as our theme verse:

> Psalm 30:5 (NASB), "[5] For His anger is but for a moment, His favor is for a lifetime; Weeping may last for the night, But a shout of joy *comes* in the morning."

- How does God move from momentary anger to lifetime favor?
- How does God move from weeping for a night to a shout of joy in the morning?

- What happens in the comma, that separates these two phrases, which is hidden to us?
- How is God's pain and grief resolved?

We shall put forth an answer to be included in the ongoing biblical conversation about reality!

Before I move into today's teaching, please allow me to give something that the Lord revealed to me this morning (10/21/2012).

I already suggested in the first sermon that in the comma between the first two phrases in Psalm 30:5, is grief. However, I'm coming to understand grief as a rite of passage, i.e. a ritual action that allows one to move from the status of denial and despair to the status of destined for God's purposes.

Grief is an in-between state, i.e. liminal state. As such it is dangerous! It's possible to defile sacred places, time, and people.

There is no safe way to move from denial and despair, except through the action and process of grief.

As we start to move into this series, we need to acknowledge the fact that the Old Testament, i.e. the foundational narratives of God's story, knows all about loss and grief.[4] **Loss and grief permeate the Old Testament stories!**

In addition, the ancient Middle Eastern Culture is a culture of grief. We probably would **not** recognize this truth, because of the variety of words used to signify grief. Beyond this barrier, we can still see ongoing instances of mourning.

> Genesis 27:41 (NASB), "[41] So Esau bore a grudge against Jacob because of the blessing with which his father had blessed him; and Esau said to himself, 'The days of mourning for my father are near; then I will kill my brother Jacob.'"

Esau observes the days of mourning or official days of grief!

We also see mourning for Jacob.

> Genesis 50:10-11 (NASB), "[10] When they came to the threshing floor of Atad, which is beyond the Jordan,

---

[4] Walter Brueggemann, *The Practice of Prophetic Imagination: Preaching an Emancipating Word*, Fortress Press, Minneapolis, Minnesota, 2012, p. 46.

they lamented there with a very great and sorrowful lamentation; and he observed seven days mourning for his father. [11] Now when the inhabitants of the land, the Canaanites, saw the mourning at the threshing floor of Atad, they said, 'This is a grievous mourning for the Egyptians.' Therefore it was named Abel-mizraim, which is beyond the Jordan."

This is the official mourning or grieving of the Hebrews which is called "sitting shiva." "Sitting shiva" is a seven-day mourning period that begins immediately after the funeral of a loved one. It is seen here and perhaps in the case of Job's three friends.

The custom of "sitting shiva" consisted of mourning with the person who was mourning by doing whatever that person wanted to do.

- If the mourning person wanted to talk, they talked.
- If the mourning person didn't want to talk, they didn't talk.

- If the mourning person wanted to cry, they cried.
- If the mourning person, wanted to laugh, they laughed.

Through the custom of "sitting shiva" the community entered into the loss, pain, and grief of the one who was suffering!

In the narrative before us, the Canaanites mistook Joseph's grieving for the grieving of Egyptians.

We also see grief at certain times when God deals with the Israelites.

> Exodus 33:1-4 (NASB), "¹ Then the Lord spoke to Moses, 'Depart, go up from here, you and the people whom you have brought up from the land of Egypt, to the land of which I swore to Abraham, Isaac, and Jacob, saying, "To your descendants I will give it." ² I will send an angel before you and I will drive out the Canaanite, the Amorite, the Hittite, the Perizzite, the Hivite and the Jebusite. ³ *Go up* to a land flowing with milk and honey; for I will not go up in your midst, because you are an

obstinate people, and I might destroy you on the way.' [4] When the people heard this sad word, they went into mourning, and none of them put on his ornaments."

Not only is the ancient Middle Eastern Culture a culture of grief, but the Old Testament writers make this culture their own. The Bible translators—which certainly includes the Old Testament—translate Hebrew and Greeks words that have to do with grief as grief, grieve, grieved, grieving, mourning, sorrow, sadness, pain, etc. Although our American eyes have difficultly seeing them, these words are everywhere in the Old Testament.

Furthermore, God's story of His interaction with His people begins with loss and grief. Abram is called to go forth from his family, country, and familiarity to a place that God would reveal to him. Abram would have to grieve the loss of his family, his country, his family religion, etc.

This grief is often seen and experienced at a personal level.

Isaac would have to grieve the sibling rivalry that led to him being tricked by his own son and the fracturing of his family.

Jacob's life was also marked by grief. He had to grieve tricking his father and brother, fleeing his home and country, never (in all probability) seeing his mother again, etc., etc., etc. However, there was one powerful grief that he refused to relinquish for a long time. It was connected to the *supposed* death of his dearly beloved son, Joseph.

> Genesis 37:35 (NASB), "[35] Then all his sons and all his daughters arose to comfort him, but he refused to be comforted. And he said, 'Surely I will go down to Sheol in mourning for my son.' So his father wept for him."

Jacob's grief seems to become a picture of the grief of the nation of Israel! All the grief of the people of Israel is represented in the life of Jacob and this symbolism is seen at various places in the Old Testament.

"By the time of Jeremiah, the imagery has moved from father Jacob to mother Rachel, but it's the same grief."[5]

> Jeremiah 31:15 (NASB), "[15] Thus says the LORD, 'A voice is heard in Ramah, Lamentation *and* bitter weeping. Rachel is weeping for her children; She refuses to be comforted for her children, Because they are no more.'"

Like Jacob, Rachel refused to be comforted. Only, this time, it is **not** Joseph who is lost, but all of the sons and daughters of Israel and Jerusalem.

During the time of Herod, the evangelist, Matthew, writes again of the weeping of Rachel. This time in the light of Herod's merciless killing of all the baby boys, two years old and under, in the vicinity.

> Matthew 2:17-18 (NASB), "[17] Then what had been spoken through Jeremiah the prophet was fulfilled: [18] 'A VOICE

---

[5] Walter Brueggemann, *The Practice of Prophetic Imagination: Preaching an Emancipating Word*, Fortress Press, Minneapolis, Minnesota, 2012, p. 46.

WAS HEARD IN RAMAH, WEEPING AND GREAT MOURNING, RACHEL WEEPING FOR HER CHILDREN; AND SHE REFUSED TO BE COMFORTED, BECAUSE THEY WERE NO MORE.'"

Jacob weeps, Rachel weeps, all of Israel weeps, the Church weeps, and even though we have seldom considered it: "God weeps!" Jewish philosopher and reform Rabbi, Emil Fackenheim wrote,

> "God Himself, as it were, weeps for His children. He weeps not for symbolic children in a symbolic exile, but for actual children in an actual exile. He weeps as would a flesh-and-blood father or mother. He weeps as Rachel does."[6]

God weeps! God weeps! God weeps!

---

[6] Emil L. Fackenhiem, "New Hearts and the Old Covenant: On Some Possibilities of a Fraternal Jewish-Christian Reading of the Jewish Bible Today," in *The Divine Helmsman: Studies on God's Control of Human Events*, Presented to Lou H. Silberman, ed. James L. Crenshaw and Samuel Sandmel (New York: KTAV, 1980), 192-193.

Now, we are becoming aware of God's grief, which is going to be the focus of my teaching. However, before we move to God's grief, let's finish discussing the fact that the Old Testament knows all about loss and grief.

If you keep reading the Old Testament, you'll come to a book that gives full expression to grief, i.e. the book of Lamentations. The word "lamentation" means a cry of sorrow or grief!

How many sermons have you heard from the book of Lamentations? Not many! When you do hear something from this sorrow filled book, it will be those portions that point to hope, without exploring or dealing with the context of loss and grief from which the hope grows.

> Lamentations 3:21-23 (KJV), "²¹ This I recall to my mind, therefore have I hope. ²² *It is of* the Lord's mercies that we are not consumed, because his compassions fail not. ²³ *They are* new every morning: great *is* thy faithfulness."

But, what about the situation that led to this wonderful pronouncement?

Lamentations 1:1-2 (NASB), "[1] How lonely sits the city That was full of people! She has become like a widow Who was *once* great among the nations! She who was a princess among the provinces Has become a forced laborer! [2] She weeps bitterly in the night And her tears are on her cheeks; She has none to comfort her Among all her lovers. All her friends have dealt treacherously with her; They have become her enemies."

The pain of the passage concerning the plight of Jerusalem is palpable, i.e. you can literally feel it like a material object.

Yes, the Old Testament is full of loss and grief. However, we are either in denial or despair because of it!

- Denial keeps us from facing the loss and doing grief work.
- Despair does the same thing, but from the opposite perspective of being negatively overwhelmed!

Even though we struggle to maintain our denial and take pills to cope with our despair, "The Day that the Earth Stood Still," 9/11/01, should be a marker that reminds us that things are **not** as they seem in America and everything has changed!

Israel also had some days that the earth stood still, such as the Fall of Jerusalem and Babylonian captivity.

Unfortunately, the dominant imagination does **not** wish to be reminded of loss and grief and will brutalize those who chose to do so.

Jeremiah Wright was **not** brutalized just because he said, "God damn America!" but because he had the audacity, the unmitigated gall to suggest that everything was **not** alright in America.

God has called me to provoke deep biblical consideration of realities that people habitually prefer not to consider. And, likewise, I will be brutalized for doing so.

Not only is the Old Testament acquainted with loss and grief, it lingers long over grief, as do its characters, i.e. Abram, Jacob, Rachel, and even God!

In Israel, loss and grief were everywhere! They were palpable and deep, yet only the prophets were willing to speak of them and only through the poetry of prophecy were they able to sound it out!

It is the duty of those who are prophetic to illuminate and illustrate loss and grief. That means it is my duty to illuminate and illustrate loss and grief!

Today, we need prophetic prophets, who understand the probability of being brutalized for raising awareness to loss and grief; **not** for the purpose of simply drawing attention to pain, but **to offer the hope of divine imagination**! I trust God that I am one of those poetic prophets?!

I still have the holy audacity to believe that there is hope for the future! This hope lies in God! This hope is **not** proclaimed in denial or in despair, but in the midst of grievous circumstances.

> Lamentations 3:21-23 (KJV), "[21] This I recall to my mind, therefore have I hope. [22] *It is of* the LORD's mercies that we are not consumed, because his compassions fail not. [23] *They are* new every morning: great *is* thy faithfulness."

It's time to begin to receive the divine revelation that hope is recalled or comes to mind in the midst of grief! When we experience the depths of grief—not the **numbness of denial** or the **immobilization of despair**, but the emotional movement of grief—we are operating on the ground of hope, because true grief can call to mind a redemptive past and points towards a liberated future!

Sermon #3

We are early in a new series on grief that was spawned by two books, *The Prophetic Imagination* and *The Practice of Prophetic Imagination*, by the German theologian, Walter Brueggemann

I was deeply impacted by these two books and the way the author talked about grief. I was particularly struck by the following quote:

> "Israel of course has a long liturgical, pastoral history of grief work in its many lament Psalms. But those laments are especially mobilized around the crisis of the fall of Jerusalem, its king, its temple, and its status as the chosen of YHWH."[7]

---

[7] Walter Brueggemann, *The Practice of Prophetic Imagination: Preaching an Emancipating Word*, Fortress Press, Minneapolis, Minnesota, 2012, p. 74.

This quote sparked a cascade of thoughts connected to grief, grief work, grief work in the Bible, the grief process, etc., etc., etc. You all know that grief has been a very important area of my theology, ministry, work, and life.

So, I began to think about our grief recovery ministry, which is called "From Midnight to Dawn." This is a metaphor of the healing that takes place when a person faithfully travels the grief recovery pathway or takes the grief recovery journey.

In *The Practice of Prophetic Imagination,* Brueggemann touches on the following psalm, which we shall use as our theme verse:

> Psalm 30:5 (NASB), "⁵ For His anger is but for a moment, His favor is for a lifetime; Weeping may last for the night, But a shout of joy *comes* in the morning."

- How does God move from momentary anger to lifetime favor?
- How does God move from weeping for a night to a shout of joy in the morning?

- What happens in the comma between the first two phrases, which is hidden to us?
- How is God's pain and grief resolved?

We shall put forth an answer to be included in this ongoing biblical conversation about reality!

Brueggemann's work is based on His study of the Old Testament prophets. In both of his books, Brueggemann works with the following thesis:

> "Prophetic preaching is an effort to imagine the world as though YHWH, the creator of heaven and earth, the Father of our Lord Jesus Christ whom we Christians name as Father, Son, and Spirit, is a real character and a defining agent in the world."[8]

Brueggemann's thesis comes from his study of the Old Testament prophets. Old Testament prophets were **not** simply predictors or social activists, but rather divine spokespersons of YHWH, who—in the light of YHWY's story—imagined the

---

[8] Walter Brueggemann, *The Practice of Prophetic Imagination: Preaching an Emancipating Word*, Fortress Press, Minneapolis, Minnesota, 2012, p. 23.

world as though YHWH was a real character and a defining agent in the world.

In the first sermon, we introduced the subject of grief.

In the second sermon, we talked about the Bible, loss, and grief.

Today, we want to deal with a problem that presents itself in this discussion, before we can deal with Old Testament prophets and their imagination for the future.

As we begin to consider the poetry and imagination of the Old Testament prophets, we notice that their writings seem to be more about divine judgment than anything else. This causes us to miss the things that the text has to say about loss, grief, compassion, etc.

Brueggemann has some powerful things to say about this, which I am only going to touch on.

First, the prophets are dealing with cause-and-effect, i.e. the consequences of choices. So, even though we do see judgment, it is <u>not</u> necessarily **divine judgment. Brueggemann makes the powerful, unlikely, and controversial contention that God does <u>not</u> often appear in judgmental utterances.** The judgment comes because the world is ordered that way. At the macro,

Newtonian level, there are some causes-and-effects. They are never as simple as they seem, but they do explain some of our observations about life.

This cause-and-effect thinking is also called retributive justice. It is an eye-for-eye or a balanced system of retribution.

This cause-and-effect thinking often causes us to miss the "therefore" in the middle of what we believe to be judgment talk. Quantum thinking or dynamic thinking would allow us to see God's compassion after the "therefore." It would allow us to see the complexity of the situation. Consider the following example.

> Malachi 3:5-6 (NASB), "⁵ 'Then I will draw near to you for judgment; and I will be a swift witness against the sorcerers and against the adulterers and against those who swear falsely, and against those who oppress the wage earner in his wages, the widow and the orphan, and those who turn aside the alien and do not fear Me,' says the LORD of hosts. ⁶ **'For I, the LORD, do not change; therefore you, O sons**

of Jacob, are not consumed" (*bold type added*).

First, we have talk of judgment!

Secondly, the talk of judgment seems to be divine, i.e. God is bringing the judgment Himself, even though the text doesn't say that directly. Nevertheless, we assume that if God is drawing near for judgment, He must be directly involved in the judgment.

Thirdly, Hebrew insiders know that judgment only comes because it is warranted. So, even if God is involved, you are judged and punished because of the consequences of your own actions and attitudes. The Hebrews don't blame God for judgment, rather they blame themselves!

Fourthly, all of this causes us to miss the divine, redemptive reversals that seem to be found in this category of texts. Even though God draws near for judgment, judgment that is deserved and connected to evil choices, there is almost always a "therefore"—in this case the word "for"—which introduces the fact that **because of His nature**, the Children of Israel were **not** consumed or destroyed in the stated judgment. So, this amounts to something more like chastisement or suspended judgment! **In the middle of this text, God turns from judgment to compassion.**

Let me restate this. God is **not** monolithic, but complex, just as we are complex. Or, we might say—more accurately—we are complex just as He is, because we are made in His image. He is not made in our image!

We all deserve judgment, because of our sinful choices and when God draws near judgment inevitably draws near also, because He is a holy and just God. However, because of the central characteristics of His character, i.e. love, generosity, and compassion, the judgment is suspended and He gives us compassion instead of the deserved judgment!

There is also an **un**intended consequence of the way we look at God, as opposed to the way the Hebrews look at God. American guilt causes us to turn away from God and stop praying to Him, because of our inadequacy, failure, sin, etc. In the light of their sin and God's nature, the Hebrews turn more quickly and deeply to God when things are more messed up!

If we considered the "therefores" of the Bible, we would see that God governs the earth and His governance is often hidden and indirect. He is **not** the King of control, but the Lord of liberty, the Master of mercy, the Ruler of redemption.

If God was directly controlling everything that goes on in the world, do you think it would look the way it looks? Me think not! I didn't say that God is not controlling anything; I said He is not controlling everything—although He is ultimately sovereign. He is working through the conventions that human choice give Him to bring His kingdom on earth, even as it is in heaven.

Brueggemann writes,

> "Of course we must accept the deep claim that 'God judges.' But clearly the matter is complex and the prophets are careful and persuasive in finding ways to mediate the claim of divine judgment in ways that take account of the real world that has irreducible moral shape."[9]

---

[9] Walter Brueggemann, *The Practice of Prophetic Imagination: Preaching an Emancipating Word*, Fortress Press, Minneapolis, Minnesota, 2012, p. 64.

In other words, God's judgment is always in the light of the real world and the morality of the world, **not** the character or personality of God.

So, divine judgment is a subset of the matter of loss. **Divine sternness is qualified by divine grief.**[10] **Because of His divine commitment to the people of Israel and the Promised Land and His centuries-long relationship with them, God cannot respond <u>in</u>differently. God is intimately involved in what happens in their history and mourns the losses! God is a relational God!**

If we were perceptive or honest, or perhaps both, we would admit the fact that this is **not** the way we see or think about God! We don't see Him as intimately involved in our affairs, mourning, and even crying over the things that happen to us! **Nevertheless, this is the way that the Old Testament repeatedly characterizes YHWH!**

Divine judgment is <u>not</u> simply a legal matter, but a <u>covenantal</u> matter. In fact, the Reformation reinterpreted Christianity in legal terms—in reaction to the Roman Catholic Church—however, "redemption" is relational from the beginning to

---

[10] Walter Brueggemann, *The Practice of Prophetic Imagination: Preaching an Emancipating Word*, Fortress Press, Minneapolis, Minnesota, 2012, p. 64.

the end, in the Bible (*Contours of Pauline Theology,* Tom Holland). To address this would take another sermon and series.

Nevertheless, the infractions and consequences of the covenant are relational. When judgment is taken at face value without reference to loss, it is misperceived as though it is a legal transaction that God has **no** stake in. It is taken as an objective fact, instead of a subjective loss that is connected to feelings—even though it may have elements of both!

God sometimes talks about judgment and punishment, but these statements are often qualified by God's grief over the loss of relationship and compassion.

It's like a person saying that s/he is going to divorce a mate because of his repeated adultery, but lamenting the fact and reminiscing about the marriage at the same time.

Again, it is one of the reasons that Old Testament prophets are poets. Poetry is the language of relationships. Proposition is the language of reason, rules, and emotional distance.

- Deuteronomy, the second giving of the law, is more propositional, but

- Genesis, God's story of His people, is narrative, drama, metaphor, and poetry.

Consequently, even though the Old Testament prophets often deal with God's anger, it is almost always in the context of losses that are connected to relational issues.
The prophets write of losses that we are all familiar with:

- "The loss of a guaranteed economy and thus job prospects;
- The loss of confidence in government, since no one knows how to cope;
- The loss of understanding between generations, exacerbated by emerging technologies;
- The loss of communication skills in a rapidly changing world;
- The loss of old moralities;
- The loss of US dominance in a world of wars we cannot win;
- The loss of conviction about exceptionalism that was, we thought, immune to violence;
- The loss of the center that no longer holds;
- The loss of old certitudes;
- The loss of a viable 'natural' environment;

- The loss of a world populated by people of 'our kind.'"[11]

Brueggemann states "That wide and deep loss generates immense anxiety that is largely amorphous and unacknowledged."[12]

Did you catch it? **There is immense anxiety or stress in America, but it is largely amorphous and unacknowledged.** What does the author mean by the word "amorphous"? The word signifies having **no** definite form or distinct shape. The immense anxiety of America is a formless mist that most people cannot put their hands on or minds around.

This immense anxiety, generated by the losses of America, is also largely **un**acknowledged. The dominant narrative, story, and language of America refuse to acknowledge the stress of our culture. **Yet, it is still real and it is still there!**

Furthermore, the dominant narrative disenfranchises or deprives loss and grief of their voting rights, because it can**not** afford to be honest. Loss

---

[11] Walter Brueggemann, *The Practice of Prophetic Imagination: Preaching an Emancipating Word*, Fortress Press, Minneapolis, Minnesota, 2012, p. 68.
[12] Ibid, p. 68.

and grief have **no** vote in our lives, because to be honest would force us to face loss and real grief!

(Donald Trump is capitalizing on the fears of Americans, but for a political purpose, not for healing or returning to God [07/23/2016]).

Disenfranchised loss and grief leads to denial! Denial is **not** the conscious refusal to face pain, but a subconscious defense mechanism that denies painful thoughts! Something clicks inside of us that keeps us from considering or facing painful thoughts.

Denial often leads to anger. When painful thoughts and feelings are pushed down inside of us, either through a voluntary or an involuntary mechanism, the result is often the processing emotion of anger!

We seem to be seeing more and more angry people!

And when anger is allowed to manifest itself, with no reference to the underlying causes and no morality to hold it in check, it often leads to violence. Our society is becoming increasingly violent.

Disenfranchised loss and grief -> denial -> numbness and/or anger -> violence

I am preaching prophetically. I am preaching so that we might acknowledge and anticipate grief. When we give loss and grief a franchise, we will give them permission to vote in our lives. When we give loss and grief a franchise, we will give them permission to be felt and embraced. When loss and grief are felt and embraced (owned), grief will transform into energy, resolve, and new possibility.[13]

Through grief, God's negative emotions are transformed into compassion and mercy!

---

[13] Walter Brueggemann, *The Practice of Prophetic Imagination: Preaching an Emancipating Word*, Fortress Press, Minneapolis, Minnesota, 2012, p. 69.

SERMON #4

We are in a new series on grief that was spawned by my reading of two books by German theologian, Walter Brueggemann: *The Prophetic Imagination* and *The Practice of Prophetic Imagination.*

I was deeply impacted by these two books and the way the author talked about grief. I was particularly struck by the following quote:

> "Israel of course has a long liturgical, pastoral history of grief work in its many lament Psalms. But those laments are especially mobilized around the crisis of the fall of Jerusalem, its king, its temple, and its status as the chosen of YHWH."[14]

---

[14] Walter Brueggemann, *The Practice of Prophetic Imagination: Preaching an Emancipating Word*, Fortress Press, Minneapolis, Minnesota, 2012, p. 74.

This quote sparked a cascade of thoughts connected to grief, grief work, grief work in the Bible, the grief process, etc., etc., etc. You all know that grief has been a very important area of my theology, ministry, work, and life. I began to think about our grief recovery ministry, which is called "From Midnight to Dawn." This is a metaphor of the healing that takes place when a person faithfully travels the grief recovery pathway or takes the grief recovery journey.

The psalm that we shall return to over and over again is

> Psalm 30:5 (NASB), "5 For His anger is but for a moment, His favor is for a lifetime; Weeping may last for the night, But a shout of joy *comes* in the morning."

In the first sermon, we introduced the subject of grief.

In the second sermon, we talked about the Bible, loss, and grief.

In the third sermon, we contrasted the ideas of God's anger and God's grief.

(So, let's take up the difficult and outlandish topic of God's grief.)

God's grief can be seen, when we consider Israel's losses. Since God's lost is connected to Israel's lost, please consider the fact that because of her disobedience and rebelliousness, Israel lost her king, her temple, her city, and confidence in the covenantal faithfulness of YHWH.

These losses are so devastating that, unless we lived at that time, we can't fully appreciate the extent of the devastation. **The only thing that probably comes close is the events of 9/11.**

Therefore, please allow me to touch on each loss.

* Israel lost her king.

  Please keep in mind that the idea of having a king was the people's, not God's! They wished to have a king to judge them like other nations. God spoke to Samuel in

  > 1 Samuel 8:7 (NASB), "⁷ The LORD said to Samuel, 'Listen to the voice of the people in regard to all that they say to you, for they have not rejected you,

but they have rejected Me from being king over them."

Evidently, having a king, made them feel equal to other nations.

Yet, God chose to use human kingship, even though He did **not** command it! This should make us cautious of attributing imperial qualities of kingship to YHWH.

- Israel lost her temple.
  The Temple of Solomon was the spiritual, religious, political, cultural center of the ancient people of Israel. It represented the height of each of these embedded institutions.
  There is no American equivalent, because these entities are embedded in one another in Israel, while they are individual institutions in America.

- Israel lost her city.
  Jerusalem was the religious, political, geographical center of the Israelites.

Spiritually, Jerusalem was the center of the social world. Ezekiel records the following:

> Ezekiel 5:5 (NASB), "⁵ Thus says the Lᴏʀᴅ GOD, 'This is Jerusalem; I have set her at the center of the nations, with lands around her.'"

Consequently, Jerusalem's capture by the Babylonians spelled **national** disaster, religious disaster, political disaster, geographical disaster, etc.

* Israel lost confidence in the covenantal faithfulness of YHWH.
  Confidence in the covenantal faithfulness of YHWH was badly shaken by the loss of their king, temple, and city to the Babylonians.

On 9/11, America lost something that was similar in importance! We lost our confidence in the fact that we are the New Jerusalem, i.e. the people and city of God who were protected by God. Although this may have never been the case, since we are more like biblical superpowers than the nation of God, yet that is what we believed! You may be **un**aware of this, but the Puritans used the language of the "New Jerusalem" concerning the founding of America. This language comes through in some of our patriotic songs,

> Mine eyes have seen the glory of the coming of the Lord:
> He is trampling out the vintage where the grapes of wrath are stored;
> He hath loosed the fateful lightning of His terrible swift sword:
> His truth is marching on.

This language amounts to the doctrine of "Manifest Destiny," which is a policy of imperialism that is rationalized as if it was God's destiny for America to rule other people. 9/11 challenged and changed all of this!

(All right, now, we're ready to attempt to recognize and feel just a little of God's grief, when His city was lost by the Israelites to various invading countries.)

In 587 BCE, when Jerusalem fell, the loss that was experienced can**not** be put into human words!

When we listen to some of the Old Testament prophets, we not only hear God's emotive reaction to Israel's losses, but the startling revelation that YHWH Himself also suffered loss. Walter Brueggemann writes,

> "The destruction of Jerusalem and the displacement of the people amounted to a huge loss for YHWH. YHWH lost **YHWH's residence** (the temple) and **YHWH's anointed agent** (the king); YHWH also lost **a covenant partner** on whom YHWH had lavished much long-term generous attention. Because of that deep loss for YHWH, the poets find that YHWH is driven to deep grief over the loss."[15]

Let's **not** go too fast! The implications of these losses are staggering!

---

[15] Walter Brueggemann, *The Practice of Prophetic Imagination: Preaching an Emancipating Word*, Fortress Press, Minneapolis, Minnesota, 2012, p. 87.

- God lost the city that He loved.
  Jerusalem was the city that God loved.

God also loves mountains and there are three biblical mountains that God seems to love: 1) Mount Moriah the site of the Temple of Solomon; 2) The Mount of Olives the site from which Jesus ascended to heaven; and 3) Mount Zion from which Jesus will one day reign. **Jerusalem rests on all three mountains.**

- God lost His home on earth.
  The Temple of Solomon was not only the religious, political, geographical center of Israel; it was the residence of YHWH. Remember God's initial instructions in

  Exodus 25:8 (NASB), "8 Let them construct a sanctuary for Me, that I may dwell among them."

  And God did dwell in the Tabernacle of Moses and in the Temple of Solomon, when His shekinah glory filled the Holy of holies!

- God lost His earthly agent.

Even though it was **not** God's plan to place a king of over Israel, because He was their redemptive and compassionate Shepherd King, once the king was in place, God anointed him and used Him as His agent. God sometimes uses human conventions that He did **not** command.

- **God also lost His wife!**
God had lavished much long-term generous attention upon His covenant partner or wife, but now she had slept with the enemy and God must divorce her. **We never talk about it this way, but we must begin to face the reality that God is a Divorcee.** God hates divorce! God did everything that He could to stay with Israel. However, in the final analysis, because of her disobedience, rebellion, and infidelity, God had to divorce her.

Any of us who have dealt with people who have experienced or are experiencing a divorce know the devastating losses that are connected to this tragedy. Divorce is called "The Never Ending Crisis." **God lost His wife!**

Brueggemann summarizes his observation and simultaneously warns us

> **"It was clear to the prophet that YHWH lingered in grief over the loss.** This point should **not** be overstated in the tradition, and prophets must have reckoned it to be a subordinate note alongside divine indignation. But it is there, and it has been largely disregarded among us"[16] (*bold type mine*).

Please allow me to recap.

- It is clear in some of the prophets' writings that YHWH lingered in grief over the losses mentioned above.
- This point should **not** be overstated, because it seems to be a note that accompanies but is subordinate to YHWH's divine righteous anger. Yet,
- In spite of its apparent subordination to YHWH's divine righteous anger, His grief has

---

[16] Walter Brueggemann, *The Practice of Prophetic Imagination: Preaching an Emancipating Word*, Fortress Press, Minneapolis, Minnesota, 2012, p. 87.

been largely disregarded by Bible readers and scholars alike.

In this series, I am correcting the general disregard for God's grief, by bringing it to the surface, looking at it more closely, and seeing what we can learn from it!

I am acting as a prophet by provoking deep biblical consideration of realities that we habitually prefer **not** to consider.

As such, I stand in a liminal, in-between, or threshold position! I am called to help people relate to God and God to interact with people! Hence, I am misunderstood and rejected by people, but unable to relate to God beyond a certain point, because of my flesh.

No sooner than Brueggemann warns us, he states that

> "The remarkable articulation by the prophets, seen most clearly by Abraham Heschel, is that YHWH's anger and indignation are interrupted

and qualified by YHWH's pathos-filled sense of loss."[17]

Abraham Heschel (January 11, 1907 – December 23, 1972) was a Polish-born American rabbi and one of the leading Jewish theologians and Jewish philosophers of the 20th century. **Brueggemann is pointing out that Heschel clearly sees the remarkable articulation of the prophets: i.e. that YHWH's anger and indignation are interrupted and qualified by His passion-filled sense of loss.** This is a profound truth, which I mentioned in the last message, but we are moving forward to take up today!

Sometimes, YHWH talks about His anger and/ or indignation, but He often interrupts that talk with pathos-filled words of loss, which eventually lead towards compassion. He starts out speaking about anger, but interrupts that talk with passion filled words of sadness and grief. These passion-filled words of sadness and grief eventually lead towards verbal and physical compassion!

---

[17] Walter Brueggemann, *The Practice of Prophetic Imagination: Preaching an Emancipating Word*, Fortress Press, Minneapolis, Minnesota, 2012, p. 87.

Jeremiah 31:20 (NASB), "[20] Is Ephraim My dear son? Is he a delightful child? Indeed, as often as I have spoken against him, I certainly *still* remember him; Therefore My heart yearns for him; I will surely have mercy on him," declares the Lord."

All of this should be shocking and new to you! It is shocking and new because we don't think of God as a person who is in dynamic relationship with us. We tend to think of Him as a concept or idea who is impassible (i.e. He has **no** feelings) and Immutable (i.e. He does **not** change). This is in spite of the fact that the Bible repeatedly refers to His feelings and the one statement about Him not changing His character is taken as a summarizing statement about His interactions, even though the Bible depicts Him as ever-changing His actions and mind.

Consequently, any feelings that the Bible attributes to Him have been explained away as anthropopathisms, i.e. God being depicted in Human emotions purely for the purpose of helping us understand Him. It is taught that God doesn't really have Human emotions. **Yet, the prophets**

treat Him as a divine person who has real feelings, even if those feelings are as high above our feelings as the heavens are above the earth.

By the way, the ancient Church Fathers never taught that God was impassible, i.e. unable to feel or interact with His Creation. What they meant by "impassible," is that God's feelings cannot be forced or manipulated by anything outside of Himself. They also taught that God was impassioned or deeply feeling and interacting with Creation (*God is Impassible and Impassioned*, Rob Lister).

To entertain God's grief, we must fight through—at least for this series—the many barriers that keep us from seeing God as capable of the emotions of anger, grief, compassion, and love. **Those who wrote the Bible had absolutely <u>no</u> problem imaging God as a passionate God!** Our modern theological inability to see God with emotions goes all the way back to the classical tradition which defined God's attributes largely in accordance with Stoic and Platonic ideas of perfection and virtue,[18] rather than in keeping with the Hebrew and

---

[18] Gregory A. Boyd, *Repenting of Religion: Turning from Judgment to the Love of God*, BakerBooks, Grand Rapids, Michigan, 2004, p. 235.

relational context of the biblical text. The Bible is a living, relational book!

Furthermore, this is new and shocking to us, because we tend to see God's anger and indignation as righteously standing alone! I wondered why Brueggemann used the words "anger" and "indignation," so I looked up both words.

- "Anger" is a strong negative emotion aroused by a real or perceived wrong.
- "Indignation" seems to suggest a righteous anger.

So, these two words describe one aspect of God's reaction to sin!

Although there is nothing in the text to suggest that YHWH's anger is **in**appropriate or that His indignation is **not** merited, God's relationship with Israel is more than a business or legal contract! **It is an emotional, blood-covenant commitment, which is frequently—if _not_ always—connected to a range of feelings from anger to compassion!**

I understand that the word "emotions" refers more to the physical, chemical, and electrical processes of the body, while "feelings" refer more to the psychological responses to those emotions, but we'll use the two words interchangeably, because that is how they are commonly used.

Anger and righteous indignation are never primary or lasting emotions with God and they are almost always balanced by His compassion, which is a primary and lasting emotion. **If we don't keep God's anger and indignation connected to His compassion, we will misperceive and distort His self-revelation!**

> Psalm 30:5 (NASB), "[5] For His anger is but for a moment, His favor is for a lifetime; Weeping may last for the night, But a shout of joy *comes* in the morning."

Please indulge me for a few moments, as I foolishly use myself as an example of these very powerful, but difficult lyrics!

When certain things happen, I get angry, but I'm **not** an angry person!

I see myself as a loving and compassionate person. However, I can get angry! Yet, my anger is almost always ameliorated, amended, or improved by my compassion.

If someone attempts to describe me only when I'm angry, they would be distorting who I really am. My anger must be seen in the light of my most dominant characteristic, i.e. my compassion.

The same is infinitely more true of God!

Furthermore, the grief that YHWH chooses to feel—because of His own loss—becomes a fulcrum, lever, or central event for newness for Israel and for YHWH. This is a fascinating metaphor of how grief is the pivotal point which leverages newness for Israel and for God![19]

---

[19] Walter Brueggemann, *The Practice of Prophetic Imagination: Preaching an Emancipating Word*, Fortress Press, Minneapolis, Minnesota, 2012, p. 88.

SERMON #5

We are engaged in a new series on grief that was spawned by my reading of two books by German theologian, Walter Brueggemann: *The Prophetic Imagination* and *The Practice of Prophetic Imagination*.

I was deeply impacted by these two books and the way the author talked about grief. I was particularly struck by the following quote:

> "Israel of course has a long liturgical, pastoral history of grief work in its many lament Psalms. But those laments are especially mobilized around the crisis of the fall of Jerusalem, its king, its temple, and its status as the chosen of YHWH."[20]

---

[20] Walter Brueggemann, *The Practice of Prophetic Imagination: Preaching an Emancipating Word*, Fortress Press, Minneapolis, Minnesota, 2012, p. 74.

This quote sparked a cascade of thoughts connected to grief, grief work, grief work in the Bible, the grief process, etc., etc., etc. You all know that grief has been a very important area of my theology, ministry, work, and life. I began to think about our grief recovery ministry, which is called "From Midnight to Dawn." This is a metaphor of the healing that takes place when a person faithfully travels the grief recovery pathway or takes the grief recovery journey.

The psalm that we shall return to over and over again is

Psalm 30:5 (NASB), "⁵ For His anger is but for a moment, His favor is for a lifetime; Weeping may last for the night, But a shout of joy *comes* in the morning."

In the first sermon, we introduced the subject of grief.

In the second sermon, we talked about the Bible, loss, and grief.

In the third sermon, we contrasted the ideas of God's anger with His grief.

In the fourth sermon, we began to explore the idea of God's grief.

(Although God's anger and grief occur together in many texts, we shall use one text in the prophecy of Hosea as an example. Before we move to the specific text that we shall work our way through, let's get some background on the prophet and God's prophecy through him.)

Hosea prophesied to the Northern Kingdom of Israel, after the split between Rehoboam, the Son of Solomon, and his enemy Jeroboam. The Northern Kingdom consisted of 10 tribes, while the Southern Kingdom was known as Judah and consisted of two tribes.

Not much information is given to us about Hosea except his credentials in the phrase "The word of the LORD which came to Hosea."

YHWH told Hosea to take a wife who was a harlot and have children by her to illustrate how the Israelites were forsaking Him. **The harlotry of Israel is spiritual infidelity.** God was Israel's true husband, but Israel was consorting with the Priests and prostitutes of the cult of Baal. Worship of this Canaanite god of fertility included sexual rites based on sympathetic magic.

Israel is depicted as God's adulterous wife, who is about to be put away (divorced), but eventually will be purified and restored (*Unger's New Bible Dictionary*).

Consequently, Hosea prophesied to the Northern Kingdom of Israel, warning her to repent of her apostasy (*falling away*) in the face of God's perpetual love for her.

What is of particular importance to us is that we get glimpses of the internal life of YHWH and the emotional journey of YHWH in His relationship with Israel!

In the 11th chapter of Hosea, the metaphor changes, but the internal life of God is the same. He moves from the metaphor of wife to the metaphor of a son. Please notice with me Hosea 11:1-9. I'll read this aloud for us.

As we explore clues to the internal life of God, we shall use Him as our supreme example of healthy grieving.

> Hosea 11:1 (NASB), "[1] When Israel *was* a youth I loved him, And out of Egypt I called My son."

The prophet, inspired by the Holy Spirit, is transmitting God's words and in those words we see some of God's feelings. God begins His statement by citing His love for the nation of Israel when he was His young son.

Can you feel God's passion? Can you relate to God's passion?

"I loved you when you were young!" "I have loved you for a long time!"

So, although—influenced by the Greek mindset—we tend to conceive of God as more of a king or ruler, He more often than **not** relates to His people (both Old Testament and NT) through His love. **His connection and interaction with His people is relational and loving!** He is their father, mother, brother, lover, husband, friend, etc.

Likewise, God, through Jesus as our Mediator, is our father, mother, brother, lover, husband, friend, etc.

In the next phrase, we get a bit of condensed history and another aspect of His relationship to Israel.

When the nation of Israel was still the 12 sons of Israel, Joseph was sold into Egypt. Down in Egypt, Joseph, the son of Israel, became the second highest ruler in the land. During this time, the children of Israel grew into the people of Israel.

Then there arose another Pharaoh who knew **not** Joseph or the things that God had wrought for Joseph's people beyond the Red Sea, i.e. before they came to reside in Egypt.

Yet, as prophesied by Jacob/Israel, God brought the people of Israel out of Egypt. God says, "I called my son out of Egypt!"

He didn't just call some people out of Egypt; He called His son out of Egypt! **Israel was the young son that He loved.** He loved Israel so much that He called him out of Egypt through 10 plagues and the destruction of much of Egypt.

God stated and demonstrated how much He loved the young nation of Israel.

God states and demonstrates how much He loves us in the NT and through the death, burial, and resurrection of His only begotten son, Jesus, the Christ!

> Hosea 11:2 (NASB), "[2] The more they called them, The more they went from them; They kept sacrificing to the Baals And burning incense to idols."

Now we come to a major problem! God seems to be saying that the more He called the Israelites, i.e. through the prophets, the more they turned from Him. **This is the beginning of God's grief in this passage.**

Feel the pain, sadness, and grief. This dearly beloved son, that God had loved from his youth and gone to great lengths to deliver from a place of bondage, would **not** heed His call, but turned away from Him.

This theme is picked up by Jesus in the New Testament, because the Israelites were still turning away from God. The title in the NASB computer Bible is "Jesus Grieves over Jerusalem." Jesus says in

> Matthew 23:37 (NASB), "37 Jerusalem, Jerusalem, who kills the prophets and stones those who are sent to her! How often I wanted to gather your children together, the way a hen gathers her chicks under her wings, and you were unwilling."

Don't miss the history of these words or the pathos they contain! God sent prophets to Israel for hundreds of years. Israel **not** only refused to listen to the prophets, they killed and stoned some of them.

The deep longing of God, in Jesus, is felt in the words

> "How often I wanted to gather your children together, the way a hen gathers her chicks under her wings, and you were unwilling."

I can see and feel the longing not only in Jesus' words, but in His body!

God is grieved over the acts of the Israelites!
God doesn't stop after pointing out that the Israelites would **not** heed His loving calls to them, but describes their behavior,

> "They keep sacrificing to the Baals and burning incense to idols!"

This son of God is breaking God's heart by treating another god as his father. After God had demonstrated His tremendous love for this son, actually over hundreds of years, His son refuses to heed His calls and worships idols to His deep grief.

Of course, this is also our story. When we refuse to listen to God, we break His heart!

(We shall get a better picture of God's inner feelings later in the text, but let's begin to deal with the grief that is bubbling to the surface here.)

God, both here and later, articulates His yearning and His grief! God yearns over Israel and He is **not** bashful about sharing this yearning.

God yearns over us and He is **not** bashful about sharing this yearning. He has loved us with an enduring love and He longs to have intimate fellowship with us!

We need to follow God's pattern, when we love someone. We should **not** be bashful in sharing our yearning to have intimate fellowship with the person that we love.

Why don't we do that? **We don't do it precisely because of what we are seeing here: the possibility of disappointment and grief!** Even if you don't know much poetry, you probably know the words of Alfred Lord Tennyson,

"Tis better to have loved and lost

Than never to have loved at all."

Likewise, both here and later, God articulates His grief. God grieves over Israel and He is **not** bashful about sharing this.

God also grieves over us, when we sin and break His loving heart! Paul writes to the Ephesians in

Ephesians 4:30 (NASB), "[30] Do not grieve the Holy Spirit of God, by whom you were sealed for the day of redemption."

Likewise, we should also be grieved—not just angry, when people we love break our hearts! Yet, it is a part of loving people. We can escape the danger, by loving no one, but we'll find that our hearts will harden and we will be dead any way!

(There are some powerful principles illustrated here. Let's begin to deal with some of them.)

Grief needs to be experienced and articulated! Who wants to experience grief? Nobody! **Yet, if we don't deal with grief, grief will deal with us!** Trying to keep grief inside is like trying to keep something in your stomach that is making you sick.

Please forgive my analogy, but it is warranted here. When I was so sick earlier this year (2012), I had extreme diarrhea and extreme vomiting.

I now suspect that my sickness was an allergic reaction to a particular blood pressure medicine. **When I took that pill, it seems that my body did everything it could to get that medication out of my system.**

One of the ways to get the poison of a broken heart out of us is to articulate it or talk about it! We have Grief ❣ Recovery classes to teach us how to talk about it! However, whether you ever work through Grief ❣ Recovery Method or not, if you want to be healthy you must follow God's lead and talk about your grief to a safe person.

Are you getting this? God's heart was broken. **It had to be a kind of midnight for God, but God moves toward dawn...God moves towards the morning!**

When our hearts are broken, we must take whatever actions that we can to move towards the dawn.

Grief signals that we know something is wrong! God acknowledged and articulated His grief, because He knew that something was wrong.

When we grieve, we signal to everyone around us, "Something is wrong!" Most of us don't want to do that, because of the repercussions of rocking the boat. We know that most people don't want us rocking the boat. Back in 1973, the Hues Corporation sang:

"Rock the Boat"
Hues Corporation

So I'd like to know where, you got the notion
Said I'd like to know where, you got the notion

To rock the boat, don't rock the boat
Rock the boat, don't tip the boat over
Rock the boat, don't rock the boat baby
Rock the boat

If we're going to get healthy, we're going to have to rock the boat!

I have said to a few people around me, "If we cared about our relationships in this church, we would grieve!" Yes, we're angry, which is one acknowledgement that things aren't right. Unfortunately, anger can be tied to superiority. We're angry about what's going on, because it's **not** right. We are **not** being treated right and we having done anything wrong. Therefore, we feel somewhat superior to the offending person.

Grief signals that something is wrong and that the griever is **not** seeking to place blame, but to acknowledge the wrong!

Grief refuses to accept the denial of reality! God could overlook the behavior of the Israelites, but He had already done that long enough. He would **not** live in denial. **Denial is a defense mechanism that denies pain!**

Many people are experts at what I call "sanctified denial." They **invoke** God, instead of **evoking** the pain. They **pray** instead of **perceiving** their pain. They refuse to face the pain of difficult situations, but spread the salve of pious statements over the grief, "God is still on the throne," "God works all things together for good," "I believe this too shall pass." **Those statements are true and helpful at the right time, but we must first face our pain.**

Pain denied produces numbness! Numbness is the context of denial. "Numb people do **not** discern or fear death.

Conversely, despairing people do **not** anticipate or receive newness."[21] They are overwhelmed by their pain and are immobilized!

So, we seek to numb ourselves with toys, amusements, food, etc. And despair immobilizes us and we can't get **up** from our fall into despair!

Brueggemann wrote, "Pain and regret denied only immobilizes.... biblical faith knows that anguish is the door to historical existence, the embrace of ending permits beginnings.... The riddle and insight of biblical faith is that awareness that 1) only anguish leads to life, 2) only grieving leads to joy, and 3) only embraced endings permit new beginnings"[22] (*numbering mine*).

1. Only anguish leads to life;
2. Only grieving leads to joy; and
3. Only embraced endings permit new beginnings (*Necessary Endings*, by Henry Cloud).

---

[21] Walter Brueggemann, *The Prophetic Imagination (Second Edition)*, Fortress Press, Minneapolis, Minnesota, 2001, pp. 59-60.

[22] Walter Brueggemann, *The Prophetic Imagination (Second Edition)*, Fortress Press, Minneapolis, Minnesota, 2001, p. 50.

Grief criticizes the status quo! Those who deny the pain of reality become numb, immobilized, and seek to maintain the status quo.

- My boss may curse at me, but I still have a job.
- My mate may be cheating on me, but it's better than being alone.
- My children may **not** be close to me, but at least they come around sometime.

Grief publicly criticizes the status quo and says, "Enough is enough! I don't want to live here any longer!

We must break with the status quo to move towards a better future! This means we must grieve. God grieves and moves towards the future and we should follow His lead!

SERMON #6

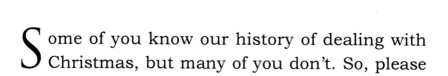

S ome of you know our history of dealing with Christmas, but many of you don't. So, please indulge me for a few moments.

In the early days of this ministry, I completely ignored Christmas. This was because of my youth, Evangelical perspectives, and disdain for the commercialization of Christmas. There were no trappings of Christmas in our church...this includes the decorations that you now see.

Pastor Jack Hayford helped me to see the importance of dealing more with the season of Christmas and re-Christianizing the trappings that have lost their origins, i.e. from candy canes to Christmas Trees. In many ways, these things point to Jesus, but have become separated from their original contexts.

Consequently, I have traditionally done a Christmas series:

- "Mary: The First Christmas Model"
- "The Gift"
- "How the Grinch Stole Christmas"
- "The Shechinah at Christmas"
- "The Alternate Reality of Christmas"
- "An Untold Christmas Story: War in the Heavens!"
- "The Expectation of the First Christmas"

However, this Christmas, I feel impressed to continue with our current series for the following reasons:

1. Our society is experiencing more and more losses with fewer tools to deal with those losses.

   I see people overwhelmed by the despair and numbed by denial on an increasing basis.

2. Holidays are connected with the "holiday blues."

"The Holiday Blues" is brought on by the feeling of being overwhelmed. We sometimes feel overwhelmed by food, people, tasks and time. This is accented by the merchandizing of the holiday and the throng of shoppers that seem to appear.

"The Holiday Blues" is also brought on by the intrusion of memories, often about friends or loved ones that have been lost.

We are all familiar with the "holiday blues," but we are probably **not** aware of how the devil plays in them. It was during the first Christmas that the devil had Herod kill an undetermined number of boy babies in Bethlehem and the surrounding environs, in an attempt to kill the Christ Child.

Think of the emotional impact upon Christmas in Bethlehem.

Likewise, every Christmas, the devil manufactures a spirit of Herod to come and kill the Christ Child in our hearts, imagination, and experience. He comes to rob us of the mystery and majesty of Christmas.

3. Furthermore, I apologize to those of you who love Christmas music.

We have fantastic musicians, but most of us play by ear, so preparing special Christmas music is extra work and energy that I sometimes don't take the time to do.

So, I'm continuing this groundbreaking series on grief that was spawned by my reading of two books by German theologian, Walter Brueggemann: *The Prophetic Imagination* and *The Practice of Prophetic Imagination.*

I was deeply impacted by these two books and the way the author talked about grief. I was particularly struck by the following quote:

"Israel of course has a long liturgical, pastoral history of grief work in its many lament Psalms. But those laments are especially mobilized around the crisis of the fall of Jerusalem, its king, its temple, and its status as the chosen of YHWH."[23]

This quote sparked a cascade of thoughts connected to grief, grief work, grief work in the Bible, the grief process, etc., etc., etc. You all know that grief has been a very important area of my theology, ministry, work, and life. I began to think about our grief recovery ministry, which is called "From Midnight to Dawn." This is a metaphor of the healing that takes place when a person faithfully travels the grief recovery pathway or takes the grief recovery journey.

The psalm that we shall return to over and over again is

Psalm 30:5 (NASB), "⁵ For His anger is but for a moment, His favor is for

---

[23] Walter Brueggemann, *The Practice of Prophetic Imagination: Preaching an Emancipating Word*, Fortress Press, Minneapolis, Minnesota, 2012, p. 74.

a lifetime; Weeping may last for the night, But a shout of joy *comes* in the morning."

In the first sermon, we introduced the subject of grief.

In the second sermon, we talked about the Bible, loss, and grief.

In the third sermon, we contrasted the ideas of God's anger with His grief.

In the fourth sermon, we began to explore the idea of God's grief.

In the fifth sermon, we began to explore God's grief in Hosea 11.

(Please notice with me Hosea 11:1-4.)

Hosea 11:3 (NASB), "³ Yet it is I who taught Ephraim to walk, I took them in My arms; But they did not know that I healed them."

Last time, we dealt with God's yearning for and grieving over Israel. He was grieving because after all that He had done for his son Israel, even from his youth up, he refused to heed His calls or return to Him.

In this verse, he returns to reminiscing about His relationship with the rebellious, but beloved nation of Israel. YHWH **not** only grieves, but He protests against the response of His beloved son. He says,

> "The Israelites won't respond to my calls, yet it was I who taught them to walk!"

Ephraim is one of the sons of Joseph and is used here to refer to the Israelites. Note the tenderness with which God refers to Israel. He taught him to walk as a doting father teaches his toddler to walk.

- He taught him to walk as a people.
- He taught him to walk with Him.
- He taught him to walk through all kinds of obstacles.
- He taught him to walk.

Not only did He teach him to walk, but, He took him in His arms! Either he lovingly picked

Ephraim up in His arms or He led him by the arms, as He taught him to walk. **In either case, a loving image is portrayed.**

- **God loves us tenderly and fervently!**
- **God teaches us to walk like a father teaches a toddler to walk.**
- **God catches us when we fall!**

Unfortunately, the people of Israel did **not** discern the divine providence of His love! Providence is God working in the details of the lives of those whom He loves with covenant love. **They did <u>not</u> know that God was taking care of them and healing them.**

- Is a toddler aware of the providence of the parent?
- Doesn't the toddler think that s/he can walk without assistance?
- Does the toddler know that his father is walking behind him and holding him up?
- Or, is that invisible to the toddler?
- Do we know that God tenderly loves us?
- Do we know that God is teaching us how to walk?

- **Are we aware of His blessings and healings or do we call them luck?**

There is something else here that is seldom pointed out. **God had a dream for Israel.** God's dream for Israel is a biblical dream and a future imagination for His son. Jeremiah speaks God's Words in

> Jeremiah 29:10-11 (KJV), "¹⁰ For thus saith the LORD, That after seventy years be accomplished at Babylon I will visit you, and perform my good word toward you, in causing you to return to this place. ¹¹ For I know the thoughts that I think toward you, saith the LORD, thoughts of peace, and not of evil, to give you an expected end."

Like Hosea, the context of God's Words through Jeremiah is, falling away, captivity in Babylon, chastening, and the imagination of their return! This is no positive announcement for a God-honoring son, but a positive announcement of a prodigal son who had spit in His face and said, "I wish that you were dead so I can have my inheritance."

I use the KJV, in this case, because the translation of the phrase "I know the thoughts I have toward you" is closer to the Hebrew syntax and culture. The American syntax and culture is deterministic and Newtonian. It has to do with plans, blueprints, and determinism, while the Hebrew word translated "thought" suggests thoughts, imagination, purposes, intention, etc. **The word "thought" seems more connected to what God would like to do, if the Israelites would cooperate!** It has more to do with the co-creation of the future, than a future that has all been planned out.

It has to do with "imagination." Doctor Stuart Brown, in his book *Play: How it Shapes the Brain, opens the Imagination, and Invigorates the Soul*, writes, "Imagination is perhaps the most powerful human ability. It allows us to create simulated realities that we can explore without giving up access to the real world."[24] We all entertain fantasies that we would never share with anyone else! We need to entertain godly fantasies!

---

[24] Stuart Brown with Christopher Vaughn, *Play: How it Shapes the Brain, Opens the Imagination, and Invigorates the Soul*, Avery, New York, New York, 2009, p. 86.

This does **not** mean that an **omni**competent God is completely thwarted by the Israelite's lack of cooperation. Unfortunately, what He can accomplish with their cooperation is different from what He can accomplish without their cooperation!

Be that as it may, God had a prophetic imagination or dream for Israel, but he refused to follow Him or return to Him, when He called. Can you feel the grief in all of this?

As a parent, can you relate to tenderly loving a child from birth to adulthood only to have that child blatantly turn from your love?

Similarly, God had dreams for America! He nurtured us in our infancy, but now we have gone astray. His heart must be utterly broken!

In addition, in keeping with the Hebrew culture of the Bible, God has a dream for The House of the Lord.

Furthermore, God has dreams for each one of us, in conjunction with our church. Consider how our sins must break His heart. **Sin is not a matter of transgressing a law, but of breaking the heart of the Father!**

Hosea 11:4 (NASB), "[4] I led them with cords of a man, with bonds of love,

And I became to them as one who lifts the yoke from their jaws; And I bent down *and* fed them."

In this verse, God changes metaphors. He moves from the metaphor of a beloved son to a beast of burden, perhaps an ox. **Our Heavenly Father mixes metaphors, as He speaks passionately about His beloved wife, son, and ox.**

The image of an ox doesn't sound loving to us, because we don't understand the importance of an ox in ancient Israel's agricultural society.

It is transparent to us that these animals were not just farm tools, but also domestic animals like dogs and cats are to us.

Furthermore, there are some outstanding contrasts that God wants to point out between animals and humans.

Animals don't have the sense that Human Beings have. However, animals often know more by instinct, than we know by intelligence and discernment. God ***lamented*** or ***grieved*** in

Isaiah 1:3 (NASB), "³ An ox knows its owner, And a donkey its master's manger, *But* Israel does not know, My people do not understand."

- An ox knows its owner, but Israel didn't know its owner.
- A donkey knows where to go to get fed, but Israel doesn't know where to go to get fed.

These domestic animals knew something by instinct that God's ancient people did not know. **God says, "I led them with cords of a man."** The NRSV says "cords of human kindness." Even when referring to Israel as an animal, God's mode of operation does **not** change. **They may operate as a beast, but He treats them with human kindness. Sin makes us like beasts, but this never changes God's love and compassion!**

God says, "I led them with bonds of love." He led them with ropes of kindness, instead of ropes of harshness!

God says, "I became to them as one who lifts the yoke from their jaws." Instead of yoking them with the burdens, He lifted the yoke of burdens from their jaws.

God says, "I bent down and fed them." He didn't throw them feed from a position of distance and superiority. He bent down and fed them!

The God that we serve is a deeply intimate and loving God! We may act like brute beasts, but He relates to us with 1) cords of human kindness, 2) ropes of love, 3) lifted burdens, and 4) intimate feedings! Wow!

(In verses 5-7, we come to a change in direction.)

> Hosea 11:5-7 (NASB), "⁵ They will not return to the land of Egypt; But Assyria—he will be their king Because they refused to return *to Me*. ⁶ The sword will whirl against their cities, And will demolish their gate bars And consume *them* because of their counsels. ⁷ So My people are bent on turning from Me. Though they call them to *the One* on high, None at all exalts *Him*."

The movement from verses 1-4 to verses 5-7 seems abrupt to me. However, that is because I have a Greek-oriented perception of God's character. I see Him as objective, logical, sequential, etc. However, God is speaking as

- A betrayed Husband;
- A rejected Father; and
- A bitten Animal Lover.

God is yearning, rejected, wounded, saddened, grieving, etc. As such, His being and His words are filled with emotion. Because God is hurting, He may seem to jump from one subject to another, but emotion is **not** logically expressed.

So, God turns from warmly reminiscing and grieving to the chastening that is coming. These words concerning chastening seem to be stated in anger.

- What husband would not be angry about a repeatedly adulterous wife?
- What father would not be angered by the rejection of a son that he has tenderly loved?
- What animal lover would not be angry about being bitten by a dog that s/he has lovingly tended?

Now, we have a number of problems!

First, we have a great deal of difficulty seeing God as having emotions. Yet, over and over in the text of the Bible, God depicts Himself as having emotions.

Secondly, because He has feelings does <u>not</u> mean that He is irrational or whimsical. Feelings often frighten us, because we know how irrational, unreasonable, and cruel humans can be when they are driven by feelings. However, Dr. Bruce Perry, in his outstanding book *Born for Love: Why Empathy is Essential—and Endangered*, points out that it is also important to note that the various regions of the brain work in concert, "**so it is impossible to actually separate 'rational thought' from emotion.** Even the most sophisticated decisions and analyses require positive and negative emotion; otherwise, it is impossible to determine which choice or idea is 'better' and which isn't. Valuing anything—even an idea—as 'good' or 'bad' requires feelings."[25]

Since, we are made in the image of God—even though His ways are as high above our ways as the heavens are above the earth—God operates

---

[25] Maia Szalavitz and Bruce D. Perry, *Born for Love: Why Empathy is Essential—and Endangered*, William Morrow, New York, New York, 2010, p. 18.

through emotion and logic. He acknowledges His feelings, articulates them, works through them, and properly processes them. He does **not** deny them, which is when they go underground and often continue to impact us and then often come out sideways in irrationality, unreasonableness, anger, cruelty, violence, etc.

In addition, the early Church Fathers taught that God is "impassible," by which they meant that God's feelings could **not** be manipulated by anyone or anything outside of Himself. They actually taught that God was impassible but also impassioned or deeply passionate (*God is Impassible and Impassioned*, Rob Lister).

Thirdly, to acknowledge feelings doesn't mean that we are driven by feelings, and God is <u>not</u> driven by His feelings!

So, the talk of chastening or punishment is <u>not</u> out of place here. Yet, God emotionally moves from love, to grief, to anger and then miraculously to compassion! Have you ever heard a jilted wife say,

> "I love my husband! We've experienced some very good times together. How could he do this to me! I feel like killing

him! I wonder if there's still a chance
for us. I wonder how he's doing?"

Now, here's the big point of the entire series:

"God's chastening, punishment, and
anger is always in the context of
and mediated by His tender love and
His grief!"

**This is what we have missed—and missing
it has caused us to misread and misjudge
God's anger!**
Because God has emotions, He gets angry—
but, God is **not** an angry God!

Psalm 30:5 (NASB), "⁵ For His anger
is but for a moment, His favor is for
a lifetime; Weeping may last for the
night, But a shout of joy *comes* in the
morning."

- God knows how to feel and show His love.
- God knows how to express and process
  His anger.

- God knows how to feel and dissipate His anger.
- God knows how to acknowledge and articulate His grief.
- God knows how to move from grief to compassion!

In our next sermon, we shall move on to consider God's possible chastening, punishment, and anger in verses 5-7.

SERMON #7

B ecause of how the Bible depicts God's grief, the losses of America, and "the holiday blues," we are continuing our groundbreaking series on grief that was spawned by my reading of two books by German theologian, Walter Brueggemann: *The Prophetic Imagination* and *The Practice of Prophetic Imagination.*

I was deeply impacted by these two books and the way the author talked about grief. I was particularly struck by the following quote:

> "Israel of course has a long liturgical, pastoral history of grief work in its many lament Psalms. But those laments are especially mobilized around the crisis of the fall of Jerusalem, its king, its

temple, and its status as the chosen of YHWH."[26]

This quote sparked a cascade of thoughts connected to grief, grief work, grief work in the Bible, the grief process, etc., etc., etc. You all know that grief has been a very important area of my theology, ministry, work, and life. I began to think about our grief recovery ministry, which is called "From Midnight to Dawn." This is a metaphor of the healing that takes place when a person faithfully travels the grief recovery pathway or takes the grief recovery journey.

The psalm that we shall return to over and over again is

> Psalm 30:5 (NASB), "⁵ For His anger is but for a moment, His favor is for a lifetime; Weeping may last for the night, But a shout of joy *comes* in the morning."

---

[26] Walter Brueggemann, *The Practice of Prophetic Imagination: Preaching an Emancipating Word*, Fortress Press, Minneapolis, Minnesota, 2012, p. 74.

In the first sermon, we introduced the subject of grief.

In the second sermon, we talked about the Bible, loss, and grief.

In the third sermon, we contrasted the ideas of God's anger with His grief.

In the fourth sermon, we began to explore the idea of God's grief.

In the fifth sermon, we began to explore God's grief in Hosea 11.

In the sixth sermon, we continued to explore God's grief and its connection to anger.

(Please notice with me Hosea 11:1-7.)

> Hosea 11:1-7 (NASB), "[1] When Israel *was* a youth I loved him, And out of Egypt I called My son. [2] The more they called them, The more they went from them; They kept sacrificing to the Baals And burning incense to idols. [3] Yet it is I who taught Ephraim to walk, I took them in My arms; But they did not know that I healed them. [4] I led them with cords of a man, with bonds of love, And I became to them as one

who lifts the yoke from their jaws; And I bent down *and* fed them. [5] They will not return to the land of Egypt; But Assyria—he will be their king Because they refused to return *to Me.* [6] The sword will whirl against their cities, And will demolish their gate bars And consume *them* because of their counsels. [7] So My people are bent on turning from Me. Though they call them to *the One* on high, None at all exalts *Him.*"

In our last message, we explored the loving relationship that God demonstrated towards Israel and began to deal with the main point of this series:

"God's anger, chastening, and punishment are always in the context of and mediated by His tender love and His grief!"

This is slightly different from what you have in your notes, because I'm continuing to work on this thesis.

First, we have a great deal of difficulty seeing God as having emotions. Yet, over and over in the text of the Bible, God depicts Himself as having emotions. Even though His ways and feelings are as high above ours as the heavens are above the earth, yet He still has feelings.

Secondly, because He has feelings does not mean that He is irrational or whimsical. Feelings often frighten us, because we know how irrational, unreasonable, and cruel people can be when they are driven by feelings.

Yet, not all people are so driven and God is certainly not driven by His feelings. He acknowledges them, articulates them, works through them, and properly processes them. He does **not** deny them, which is when they go underground, but later come out sideways.

So, talk of chastening or punishment is not out of place here. Yet, God emotionally moves from love, to grief, to anger and then miraculously to compassion! Have you ever heard a jilted husband say,

"I love my wife! We've experienced some very good times together. How could she do this to me! I want her to hurt like I hurt! I wonder if there's still a chance for us. I wonder how she's doing?"

Remember: this is God's experience leading up to the divorce!
Because we have missed God's compassion, grief, and conflicting feelings, this has caused us to misread and misjudge God's anger.

(Now, let's go back to verse 5.)

Hosea 11:5 (NASB), "⁵ They will not return to the land of Egypt; But Assyria—he will be their king Because they refused to return *to Me*."

YHWH now turns from warmly reminiscing about and grieving over His rebellious son, to talking about chastening or punishment. Some scholars say this is about punishment, but I prefer to think of it as chastening, with that chastening coming from God stepping back as opposed to Him directly doing the chastening.

First, I see this as chastening rather that punishment, because of God's relationship to

Israel and the mercy that He has on His children. The writer of the Hebrews wrote in

> Hebrews 12:4-6 (NASB), "⁴ You have not yet resisted to the point of shedding blood in your striving against sin; ⁵ and you have forgotten the exhortation which is addressed to you as sons, 'MY SON, DO NOT REGARD LIGHTLY THE DISCIPLINE OF THE LORD, NOR FAINT WHEN YOU ARE REPROVED BY HIM; ⁶ FOR THOSE WHOM THE LORD LOVES HE DISCIPLINES, AND HE SCOURGES EVERY SON WHOM HE RECEIVES.'"

He may punish or condemn the wicked and sinners, but **those that God loves, He disciplines!** The author is quoting

> Proverbs 3:12 (NASB), "¹² For whom the LORD loves He reproves, Even as a father *corrects* the son in whom he delights."

Have you ever experienced God's chastening? I have!

In his first letter to the Corinthians, Paul explains that we should **not** take the Lord's Supper with unconfessed sin in our lives. We should judge ourselves, by repenting and confessing our sins. However, if we don't judge ourselves through repentance and confession, then God will have to judge us, but consider what he says about this situation.

> 1 Corinthians 11:32 (NASB), "[32] But when we are judged, we are disciplined by the Lord so that we will not be condemned along with the world."

So, what YHWH is discussing is chastening, not punishment! God never punishes His Children. Punishment involves condemnation! God punishes the world, but He chastens His children. The definition of the word "punish" is the requiring of compensation for wrong doing. Since there is **no** way for the world to pay for their sin, they must experience the sentence that is attached to their punishment.

Condemnation is the declaration of guilt or wrong doing. God, because He is just, must declare all of us guilty of sin and sentence us to death and hell. But praise God that the condemnatory sentence that accompanies sin has been paid for because of God's Favor and through the substitutionary payment of Jesus, the Christ.

In the Old Testament, the payment is made looking **forward** to the cross. In the Second Testament, the payment is made looking **back** to the cross.

Therefore, we can never be punished along with the world, because our condemnatory sentence has been paid for by our Lord and Savior, Jesus, the Christ, in keeping with God's favor!

Furthermore, the Hebrews see God as doing everything, yet they don't blame God, because they take responsibility for their choices. Putting this in my own words, I would say

"God is involved in everything that goes on in our lives, but He does **not** cause everything!"

Brueggemann makes the excellent point that the Old Testament prophets "know the name of the One who governs, even if that governance remains hidden and indirect."[27] That is what I see in the texts of the Bible, i.e. that God **governs** in a more hidden and indirect way rather than **reigns** in a visible, direct way. God's more direct and visible reign is coming, but it's **not** here yet!

So, in this text, God is talking about the chastening that His rebellious son is about to experience, when He steps back and allows him to experience the consequences of his turning away from Him.

When you have children, sometimes your chastening is to simply let them experience the consequences of their choices!

Modern parents are often too co-dependent to allow chastening to do its work in the lives of their children. Hence, children often never grow up, because all of their consequences are kept from them by hovering parents. This is called spoiling a child and one expert said that spoiling a child is child abuse, because it is setting the child up for a world that does **not** exist.

---

[27] Walter Brueggemann, *The Practice of Prophetic Imagination: Preaching an Emancipating Word*, Fortress Press, Minneapolis, Minnesota, 2012, p. 61.

For example, we shelter our children from the consequences of their tardiness, but their employers won't do that!

We make excuses for them when they steal their friend's toys, but the law won't do that, when they are adults.

We side with them when their marriages are difficult, but the courts won't do that.

God says, "They will not return to the Land of Egypt, but to Assyria." The *Word Biblical Commentary* says that this is curse language. So, this action is the result of their breaking the covenant. **<u>Therefore, it is the consequences of breaking the covenant.</u>**

Egypt is a symbol of the Israelite's long-time bondage! They were once enslaved in Egypt, but God delivered them.

Because they had turned from God and would <u>not</u> turn back to Him, they would <u>not</u> return to Egypt again, but to Assyria. Even though they were enslaved in Egypt, it was **not** because of sin, but rather because of circumstances. However, because of their sin, they would **not** return to the **circumstantial slavery** of Egypt, but the **deserved slavery** of Assyria.

Assyria would be Israel's king, because the nation refused to return to God. God was his King, but he refused to heed God's call or turn to Him. This is actually a play on the Hebrew word for "turn." It is more literally,

> "Israel will **not** turn to Egypt, but to Assyria, it will be His king, because Israel refused to turn to me!"

(All right, let's go to the next verse.)

> Hosea 11:6 (NASB), "[6] The sword will whirl against their cities, And will demolish their gate bars And consume *them* because of their counsels."

Again, as Hosea gives voice to God's perspectives, it's interesting that God does **not** say that I will destroy you or devour you. He doesn't even use the divine passive. The divine passive is when there is **no** agent to an action. In that case, the verse would likely read,

> "your cities will be destroyed because of your counsels."

When there is **no** agent to a biblical action, it is assumed that God is the Agent.

For instance, in Mark 2:5, Jesus says to the paralytic,

> "Son, your sins are forgiven."

The verb "forgiven" is in the passive voice. Jesus doesn't say,

> "Son, God has forgiven you for your sins."

However, the agent of this divine passive is God!

Yet, here, God—through Hosea—says to the Israelites,

> "The sword will whirl against their cities."

God is <u>not</u> the agent of Israel's chastening, but rather the sword of the Assyrians. Some may argue that God **sent** the Assyrians, but it could also be argued that God simply stepped back and allowed the Assyrians to do what they naturally do.

Nevertheless, God is willing to talk about the chastening of His son, because of His son's rejection and rebellion, and that chastening will come through war with the Assyrians.

Don't we naturally engage in the same kind of angry talk and imagination when we are rejected! **Yet, it is often just talk and imagination!** We say, "I'm going to cuss him out when I see him." "I'm going to jump on her when I see her!" Yet, most often we don't. It's just angry talk! And angry talk and imagination is natural, when we have been wronged!

The Assyrians will demolish the gate bars of Israel, i.e. the Assyrians will breach the fortifications of the cities of Israel. And once they have breached the fortifications of Israel's cities, they will consume the inhabitants of Israel.

God adds that the Assyrians will demolish their gate bars, breach their cities, and consume them, because of their counsels. It seems that God is referring to the false prophets, who were prophesying good things for Israel, instead of warning them to return to God.

(Let's touch on one more verse.)

Hosea 11:7 (NASB), "⁷ So My people are bent on turning from Me. Though they call them to *the One* on high, None at all exalts *Him.*"

The translations and scholars are divided over the translation of this verse, as they are over a number of verses in this chapter. However, we shall follow the translation of the NASB. YHWH summarizes the unfaithfulness of His dearly beloved son, Israel. He says,

"So...therefore...my people are bent on turning from me. Even though the prophets call them to me, none of them exalts me!"

God kept sending prophets to call Israel to Himself, but they would **not** heed His call. They were bent on turning away from God and they did not exalt Him as they should have!

With the direction of God's sharing, i.e. grief, chastening, anger, and stepping back, you will be shocked by what comes next, but that will have to wait until next week. However, let's just preview the next verse.

Hosea 11:8 (NASB), "⁸ How can I give you up, O Ephraim? How can I surrender you, O Israel? How can I make you like Admah? How can I treat you like Zeboiim? My heart is turned over within Me, All My compassions are kindled."

In this verse, we see in God a turn towards compassion!

Psalm 30:5 (NASB), "⁵ For His anger is but for a moment, His favor is for a lifetime; Weeping may last for the night, But a shout of joy *comes* in the morning."

In the meantime, while we wait for next week, please keep in mind that God's talk of chastening is much worse than the reality, because it is mediated by love and grief.

Also keep in mind how much God loves us, even when we are rebellious.

SERMON #8

As I tried to follow the leading of the Lord in preaching this series at this time, it coincides with the senseless and brutal slaying of children in Connecticut. As Herod killed male children in Bethlehem and its vicinity, so the Spirit of Herod has driven a young man to kill children in Connecticut. Even as the first Christmas was surrounded by grief and joy—as is life—, so this Christmas is surrounded by the grief of death and the joy of the celebration of the birth of Him who is life! Oh, how we need the salve of grief recovery today.

Therefore, by divine providence, we are continuing our groundbreaking series on grief that was spawned by my reading of two books by German theologian, Walter Brueggemann: *The*

Prophetic Imagination and *The Practice of Prophetic Imagination.*

I was deeply impacted by these two books and the way the author talked about grief. I was particularly struck by the following quote:

"Israel of course has a long liturgical, pastoral history of grief work in its many lament Psalms. But those laments are especially mobilized around the crisis of the fall of Jerusalem, its king, its temple, and its status as the chosen of YHWH."[28]

This quote sparked a cascade of thoughts connected to grief, grief work, grief work in the Bible, the grief process, etc., etc., etc. You all know that grief has been a very important area of my theology, ministry, work, and life. I began to think about our grief recovery ministry, which is called "From Midnight to Dawn." This is a metaphor of the healing that takes place when a person faithfully

---

[28] Walter Brueggemann, *The Practice of Prophetic Imagination: Preaching an Emancipating Word*, Fortress Press, Minneapolis, Minnesota, 2012, p. 74.

travels the grief recovery pathway or takes the grief recovery journey.

The psalm that we shall return to over and over again is

Psalm 30:5 (NASB), "⁵ For His anger is but for a moment, His favor is for a lifetime; Weeping may last for the night, But a shout of joy *comes* in the morning."

In the first sermon, we introduced the subject of grief.

In the second sermon, we talked about the Bible, loss, and grief.

In the third sermon, we contrasted the ideas of God's anger with His grief.

In the fourth sermon, we began to explore the idea of God's grief.

In the fifth sermon, we began to explore God's grief in Hosea 11.

In the sixth sermon, we continued to explore God's grief and its connection to anger.

In the seventh message, we explored God's talk of Israel's chastening.

Today, we come to a miraculous change in the verses that we have been studying. Please notice with me Hosea 11:1-8.

We see God's warm reminiscing about His dearly beloved Son, i.e. the nation of Israel.

We see God's pain, sadness, and grief because of the rejection and rebellion of His son.

We saw that God was a betrayed husband, a rejected father, and a bitten animal lover!

Consequently, God turns from relational and emotional talk to talk of chastisement and apparent anger.

It is at this point that something miraculous happens!

Hosea 11:8 (NASB), "[8] How can I give you up, O Ephraim? How can I surrender you, O Israel? How can I make you like Admah? How can I treat you like Zeboiim? My heart is turned over within Me, All My compassions are kindled."

At this point, a divine shift takes place! You might as well see a large, capitalized, emboldened, italicized, underlined "but" in the text! "But God...!"

The scholars of The *Word Biblical Commentary* cite the effect of punishment upon Israel as the cause of this divine shift, and that may be true. However, I see something else! Something which Evangelicals and Greek-oriented Americans cannot see or even consider. **The divine shift is an emotional shift that flows from the transformative power of grief!**

I believe it is grief that starts the journey from midnight to dawn. As YHWH lingers over His loss and fully feels His grief, a change begins to take place which is indicated in four perfectly balanced, poetic questions.

"How can I give you up, O Ephraim?"

"How can I surrender you, O Israel?"

"How can I make you like Admah?"

"How can I make you like Zeboiim?"

Before we attempt to expose the grief which underlies these four statements, please allow me to point out that the vivid backdrop of this passage is God's character! He is a loving, compassionate, merciful, forgiving, generous God! Therefore, healthy grieving has transformed His loving heart. **Instead of seeking Israel's chastening, He is moving towards limiting Israel's suffering.**

I believe grief, properly processed, will have a transformative effect upon the heart of any human being. **However, if our hearts are more like the heart of God, the transformation will be more like His, i.e. our compassion will be more divine.**

The four questions that God asks are probably Hebrew parallelism. So, the second question is a restatement and embellishment of the first and the fourth is a restatement and embellishment of the third.

"How can I give you up or surrender you Ephraim/Israel?" God can't fathom giving up on or surrendering Israel to destruction at the hands of the Assyrians! As I read the commentaries, I saw great debate. You are hardly aware of this debate, because it is a debate among scholars of different theological schools. Yet, every time you pick up a Bible dictionary, commentary, or tool, the authors give answers according to a particular school of thought.

Those who are more Calvinistic, deterministic, and conservative warn against taking this language too literally. They remind us that God can never really experience self-doubt or anxiety over issues of justice and mercy. Therefore, God has chosen these words and metaphors to simply help us understand what we really can**not** understand.

And yet, other scholars point out the emotional power of these depictions of God. **The language reveals the raw emotion of God and in this language and these metaphors the love of God is revealed.** According to my reading concerning cognitive science and neuroscience, the Bible is not mostly metaphor because humans are objective and God is just trying to help us understand Him. As human beings, we actually think, especially with respect to abstract thought, metaphorically—not objectively or subjectively (*Philosophy in the Flesh*, Lakoff and Johnson).

It's time for you to understand that many times, as humans, we are **not** interpreting the Bible, but simply reading the Bible through our cultural lenses. The conservatives read conservative bents into the text, while other read more progressive bents into the text.

It is my contention that we ought to be trying to interpret the text as close to what the original people heard when God originally spoke to

them. This means that we will need to attend to the culture of the original people. God could **not** give a word that had universal culture to us, but one that was spoken to a specific people, in a specific place, at a specific time. In this way, the entire Bible is culturally conditioned. This does not mean that God does not have the truth, but that we can't perceive that truth in a neutral fashion, because we are human beings.

We can believe anything we want to believe, but if it does **not** flow from the text, we can't call it "biblical"!

God has given us His story, so that we might understand the original words, truths, and principles of His story and then apply those principles to our times and contexts.

In the Bible,

- God is **not** a concept!
- God is **not** a statement!
- God is **not** a Greek concept of perfection!
- God is **not** a theological construct!
- God is a trustworthy and compassionate being who wants to have a deeply intimate and personal relationship and fellowship with us!

Although God never changes in compassion, He does change His mind.

Are you in any real relationships? Are you experiencing any intimate fellowship with anyone? Don't you know trustworthy people who change their minds, because of changing circumstances and considerations? Even so, God sometimes changes His mind—even though He is trustworthy, loving, compassionate, and operates with integrity.

To understand God in this text, we need to know the ancient Hebrew perspective of emotion. "The Hebrews believe in the spontaneous expression of impulses, desires, and feelings or emotions. Such behavior is normal, acceptable, and in fact expected in daily Mediterranean life. Thus, the free and unrestrained expression of emotions in all human interactions is a core value in Mediterranean culture, since it marks a person as authentically human from a Mediterranean perspective."[29]

Let me say it again, "In the Mediterranean culture behind the Bible, if you don't express your feelings you aren't authentically human."

---

[29] John J. Pilch & Bruce J. Malina, *Biblical Social Values And Their Meaning*, Hendrickson Publishers, Inc., Peabody, Massachusetts, 1993, p. 53.

That is the cultural context into which God spoke these words and probably the reason why He chose to reveal these things about Himself. **They would have great meaning to the Hebrew people**.

What does this mean to us? We live in a culture that is almost the exact opposite. We restrain our emotions and attempt to never let people see us sweat.

So, we must stretch to understand that in the Hebrew culture you are **not** human, if you don't express your emotions. **Yet, YHWH is <u>not</u> whimsical or capricious; He is appropriately and personally emotional!** He feels! He grieves! He gets angry—though He is **not** an angry God! He feels compassion! He loves!

Furthermore, appropriate and personal reminiscing, sadness, and grief have a transformative effect upon God, His hurt, and His anger. **Consequently, grief is the process that transforms sadness, anger, and negative feelings into mercy, compassion, and forgiveness! Being appropriately and personally emotional, i.e. processing loss and grief, is the pathway from the numbness of denial and the immobility of despair to practical hope for the future!**

Between verses seven and eight, in the darkness of silence, grief is transforming the emotions of God! We see the same thing in the commas of Psalm 30:5.

(Now, we're ready to try to understand more of the language in these verses.)

God can't imagine giving them up to chastening at the hands of the Assyrians.

God can't imagine surrendering them to the cruelty of the Assyrians.

"How can I treat make you like Admah and Zeboiim?" Admah and Zeboiim were two of the lesser known cities in the region of Sodom and Gomorrah. So, to treat them like Admah and Zeboiim is to destroy them or allow them to be destroyed! **God can't bring Himself to consider their destruction; whether you believe He personally brought about the destruction or stepped back and allowed them to experience the consequences of their choices.**

Remember, the Hebrews see God as the ultimate agent of all actions and yet do **not** absolve themselves of responsibility. In America, once we see God as the agent of an action, we tend to see ourselves as free of responsibility.

I don't believe the text demands that we see it exactly as the Hebrews and certainly our application of biblical principles must be different than they were 3,000 years ago. The Word of God is living and active and must be applied in each generation and context. **So, God may be saying, "He can't bring Himself to consider letting Israel be destroyed."**

Now, we come to the explicit emotionality of God,

"My heart is turned over within Me, all
My compassions are kindled!"

More literally, "His heart is changed from anger to mercy and His compassions have grown warm and tender." His true nature is allowed to come forth, because of the process that has been worked through in the text.

Properly processed grief is an energy or force that moves us towards compassion, mercy, and forgiveness. In contrast, anger is a force that moves us towards blame and distance! Properly processed grief moves us towards feeling with the perpetrator (*i.e. compassion*), leniency towards the perpetrator (*i.e. mercy*), and releasing the perpetrator from the debt we feel we are owed (*i.e. forgiveness*).

(Let's touch on the definitions of these states for a moment.)

> compassion "deep feeling for and understanding of misery or suffering and the concomitant desire to promote its alleviation : spiritual consciousness of the personal tragedy of another or others and selfless tenderness directed toward it" (*Webster's Dictionary*).

> Mercy "pity"

> Forgiveness "the releasing from a debt"

If we are properly processing our grief, the transformation will move us from hardness, anger, and unforgiveness towards 1) compassion, 2) mercy, and 3) forgiveness. **It will move us from the darkness of night towards the light of morning!**

This is particularly powerful with respect to forgiveness. We urge people to forgive, but offer them no mechanism to work this out! The Grief ❣ Recovery Method® is a mechanism of deep forgiveness!

Our Grief ❣ Recovery Program is one way to adequately process grief. However, here is an abbreviated, biblical model that I formulated.

First, let me give you a motto: "To free yourself from it, you've got to face it!" "How do you do that?"

Step #1:   Frame it.

We cannot face something that we have **not** even acknowledged. So, first we need to acknowledge the fact that someone or something has disappointed us, let us down, or hurt us. We need to frame that pain.

Step #2:   Face it.

We need to face the pain head on. We need to avoid denial or deflection and face the fact that someone very important to us has failed us.

Step #3:   Feel it.

Facing the fact that we have pain and fully feeling our pain is **not** the same thing. We need to plumb the depth of our pain. We need to go down the roller coaster of pain to the bottom. We need to grieve our pain. We need to fill up our buckets with the tears of loss. This drives us to God and God alone! He is the only One that can sustain us in true grief.

Step #4: Forsake it.

Once we have fully felt our pain, really grieved it, cried it out, we can forsake. We forsake the pain and release the person from their debt against us. When we release that person, we release ourselves from the negative bondage with that person.

Step #5: Feast about it.

Once God has brought us through the valley of the shadow of death, we need to feast about it or celebrate what God has done! Henry Mitchell, in his dynamic books on preaching, illustrates the point that celebration and experience are critically important to intuitive learning. Then intuitive learning changes our core beliefs and our behavior.

- When you have grieved, you can move on after the divorce, no matter what anybody else thinks.

- When you have grieved, you can see your ex-mate who goes to this church, without becoming depressed.
- When you have grieved, you can see your ex-mate's new mate and not be completely undone.

Even though God may be grieving, angry, hurt, and stepping back, He won't fully give us up to the chastening for our sins and rebellion, because He's a compassionate God. He has paid the price for our sins and He processes His anger so that

> Psalm 30:5 (NASB), "⁵ For His anger is but for a moment, His favor is for a lifetime; Weeping may last for the night, But a shout of joy *comes* in the morning."

SERMON #9

The nation seems to be in grief over the Newtown, Connecticut shooting. The shooting seems to be in keeping with the spirit of Herod, which is the demonic spirit that compelled Pharaoh to kill male babies in Egypt and Herod to kill all of the male infants in Bethlehem and the surrounding environs, during the first Christmas.

So, my sermon series is providentially timely.

We are ending a groundbreaking series on grief that was spawned by my reading of two books by German theologian, Walter Brueggemann: *The Prophetic Imagination* and *The Practice of Prophetic Imagination.*

I was deeply impacted by these two books and the way the author talked about grief. I was particularly struck by the following quote:

"Israel of course has a long liturgical, pastoral history of grief work in its many lament Psalms. But those laments are especially mobilized around the crisis of the fall of Jerusalem, its king, its temple, and its status as the chosen of YHWH."[30]

This quote sparked a cascade of thoughts connected to grief, grief work, grief work in the Bible, the grief process, etc., etc., etc. You all know that grief has been a very important area of my theology, ministry, work, and life. I began to think about our grief recovery ministry, which is called "From Midnight to Dawn." This is a metaphor of the healing that takes place when a person faithfully travels the grief recovery pathway or takes the grief recovery journey.

The psalm that we have returned to over and over again is

Psalm 30:5 (NASB), "⁵ For His anger is but for a moment, His favor is for

---

[30] Walter Brueggemann, *The Practice of Prophetic Imagination: Preaching an Emancipating Word*, Fortress Press, Minneapolis, Minnesota, 2012, p. 74.

a lifetime; Weeping may last for the night, But a shout of joy *comes* in the morning."

In the first sermon, we introduced the subject of grief.

In the second sermon, we talked about the Bible, loss, and grief.

In the third sermon, we contrasted the ideas of God's anger with His grief.

In the fourth sermon, we began to explore the idea of God's grief.

In the fifth sermon, we began to explore God's grief in Hosea 11.

In the sixth sermon, we continued to explore God's grief and its connection to anger.

In the seventh message, we explored God's talk of Israel's chastening.

In the eighth message, we began to see how properly processed grief brought about a divine transformation in God.

Today, we are giving final attention to the miraculous change in the verses that we have been studying. Please notice with me Hosea 11:1-9.

We see God's warm reminiscing about His dearly beloved Son, i.e. the nation of Israel.

We see God's pain, sadness and grief because of the rejection and rebellion of His son.

God is a rejected father, a jilted husband, and a bitten animal lover!

God turns from relational and loving talk to emotional talk of anger and chastisement.

Then, we see God shift from talk of anger and chastisement, because of a change that is facilitated by grief. He wrestles with giving Israel up and treating him like other nations that had been destroyed.

> Hosea 11:9 (NASB), "⁹ I will not execute My fierce anger; I will not destroy Ephraim again. For I am God and not man, the Holy One in your midst, And I will not come in wrath."

From the beginning of this series, I have been postulating God's anger. I have **not** treated His anger as a fact, because we have taken the text as it was written, rather than jumping ahead.

Now, YHWH mentions His anger. He is **not** just angry; He is fiercely angry! The word "fierce" is more literally "burning." **God had burning anger or in modern parlance, "God was hot!"**

Why wouldn't He be hot? His son, whom he had tenderly loved from His youth, had rebelled against Him and refused to heed his call and turn back to Him.

Israel, whom He had given birth to and loved tenderly for hundreds of years, had turned to idol gods. When God called to Israel, the nation refused to respond to His call and continued to choose idol gods over Him.

This precipitated reminiscing.

This precipitated sadness.

This precipitated grief.

This precipitated Him stepping back from Israel.

This precipitated anger.

God gets angry, but He is <u>not</u> an angry God! Anger is something He feels from time-to-time, when provoked, but it is **not** a permanent part of His nature, character, or attributes.

It's all right to get angry! Paul wrote to the Ephesians in

Ephesians 4:26 (NASB), "²⁶ BE ANGRY, AND *yet* DO NOT SIN; do not let the sun go down on your anger."

Anger can be useful in some situations, particularly when movement out of a negative situation is needed.

Yet, anger is transformed into compassion through properly processed grief. **The movement from anger to compassion is a divine and redemptive reversal! We expect to see the pain of anger and chastisement, but instead experience the redemptive reversal of compassion, mercy and forgiveness!**

Now, God's whole posture is changed,

"I will not destroy Ephraim again!"

Grief has attenuated and transformed His stance. He has moved from talking about chastening and anger to compassion, pity, and forgiveness!

He doesn't stop there, but gives us the basic reason why He is able to change,

"He is God and not a man. He is the
Holy One who dwells in their midst and
He refuses to come in wrath!"

Men come in wrath, but God is **not** angry or vengeful! Men are unholy, but He is holy! Anger can create **im**personality and distance, but God is **not** separated from them. He is dwelling in their midst. **Because of who He is, i.e. His character, He simply refuses to come in wrath.** The word "wrath" is more literally excitement or anguish.

Yes, God has emotions, but His emotions don't rule Him! Because He has properly grieved the offense, those emotions have dissipated and been replaced by more tender emotions. Because He is impassible, i.e. no emotions can be forced upon Him, He has chosen compassion.

Grief energizes the new order! Grief allows God to say,

"Behold, I do a new thing!" (Isaiah 43:19)

When the pain has been felt and processed, energy can arise from the ashes!

Grief energizes because it causes people to engage the promise of newness that is at work in the history of our God. Once we have given up hope in the old stuff, we're ready for promises of new beginnings! Henry Cloud said, in *Necessary Endings*, we have to get hopeless about things that offer false promises!

God's character is **not** the only reason why God's anger is transformed to compassion. Another reason is His relative position to Israel. **He is in their midst!** He is in intimate fellowship with them and cannot act as if He is disconnected or distant.

It's easier to be angry with people that we don't have to interact with, but much harder when we come face-to-face with those same people.

Praise God, that He lives inside of us—in the person of the Holy Spirit—and therefore cannot act disinterested, disconnected, or distant!

(But there's even more here!)

Grief allowed God to trust in His own goodness and compassion!

For us, grief audaciously dares to trust God! To grieve, I have to trust that God will take me through it and that God has something better for me beyond it!

Now, back to our theme verse:

Psalm 30:5 (NASB), "⁵ For His anger is but for a moment, His favor is for a lifetime; Weeping may last for the night, But a shout of joy *comes* in the morning."

Now, through of our study of Hosea 11:1-9, we can see what happened in the comma between night and morning! In these lyrics, David puts forth a general truth about God. This general truth is deduced from God's actions in all of the stories of His dealings with His people, in the Old Testament.

His anger is but for a moment! Well, if I read some of the scholars and commentaries of today, I would believe that His anger is persistent. Yet, David teaches us through these divine song lyrics that God's anger is but for a moment. Israel's sins were certainly longer than a moment. Israel's sins were persistent, but God's anger is but for a moment. Why? The answer is in the comma!

- In that comma is the processed grief.
- In that comma is the movement from the moment to the lifetime.
- In that comma is the divine shift from anger to favor.
- In that comma is the transformation of God from momentary anger to lifetime favor!"

Because God is a loving, compassionate, merciful, forgiving, generous God, His favor is for a lifetime. The thing that allows Him to **demonstrate** that favor is processed grief!

"Weeping may last for the night." When there is rebellion, rejection, idolatry, sin, etc., there is going to be some weeping. David doesn't tell us who is weeping, but the first lyrics are about God. While the second set of lyrics could be about people, it is plausible that they are also about God. When His heart is broken, He is going to weep. Yet, weeping is **not** where He lives and is **not** permanent. Weeping may last for the night. **However, God weeps through the night!**

Now, let's **not** minimize the night, for though it is but one night, it can seem like a never ending night. Have you ever wondered like David, "How long Oh LORD?"

Yet, comma, "but," comma, "a shout of joy comes in the morning!" **The comma and the "but" are where grief is processed. Grief is the energy or force that facilitates God's movement from weeping to shouting, from nighttime to the dawn of morning, from the darkness of the night to the light of the morning.**

God weeps through the night, but God gives a shout of joy in the morning! The phrase "shout of joy" is the word *rinnah*. It comes from the Hebrew word *ranan*. It is an onomatopoetic word that suggests resounding or Making an ear splitting nananana noise. In the morning, God splits the ear by saying, "Nananananananana...."

Grief recognizes the end of the present order, i.e. the order of sin, rejection, and rebellion, anger and weeping, night and darkness. In grief, God is moving on from the night to the morning. When we grieve, we recognize the end of the present order. The things that bring reminiscing, sadness, grief, and anger are coming to an end.

Grief will mean necessary endings! Endings are a natural part of the universe, and your life and business must face them, stagnate, or die.[31] **The good cannot begin, until the bad ends!**[32] "Getting to the next level always requires ending something, leaving it behind, and moving on. **Growth itself demands that we move on.** Without the ability to end things, people stay stuck, never becoming who

---

[31] Henry Cloud, *Necessary Endings: The Employees, Businesses, and Relationships that All of us Have to Give Up in Order to Move Forward*, HarperCollinsPublishers, New York, New York, 2010, p. xiii.

[32] Ibid, p. 1.

they are meant to be, never accomplishing all that their talents and abilities should afford them."[33]

When you work through necessary endings, you'll need to deal with three kinds of people: the wise person, the fool, and the evil person. Identifying the kind of person you're dealing with is important, because you cannot deal with everyone in the same way. These labels are **not** rigid, but helpful ways to identify particular patterns.

"When truth presents itself, the wise person sees the light, takes it in, and makes adjustments."[34] **Talk to him or her!**

"The fool tries to adjust the truth so he does not have to adjust to it."[35] **Stop talking to him or her. Talking only makes things worse.**

"Evil people mean to harm you." **Protect yourself by getting yourself a lawyer, a gun, and some money.**

God knows who we are and how to deal with us!

Now we can summarize what we have learned from exploring God's grief in Psalm 30:5 and Hosea 11:1-9.

---

[33] Ibid, p. 7.
[34] Ibid, p. 127.
[35] Ibid, p. 133.

- The way God processes His grief is an example of the way we need to process our grief.
- Grief needs to be articulated and experienced!
- Grief signals that we know something is wrong!
- Grief refuses to accept the denial of reality!
- Grief criticizes the status quo!
- Grief, properly processed, transforms loss, pain, and anger into compassion, mercy, and forgiveness.
- Grief recognizes the end of the present order!
- Grief energizes the new order!
- Grief dares to trust in God!
- Grief facilitates our movement from midnight to dawn.

Books by the Author:

The Church: The Family of Families
God is Greater than Family Mess
The Eight Ministries of the Holy Spirit
The Eight Ministries of the Holy Spirit Workbook
The Biblical World through New Glasses
Lord of the Flies: A Leadership Fable
Grief: A Biblical Pathway to God

CPSIA information can be obtained
at www.ICGtesting.com
Printed in the USA
FFOW01n1945030217
32076FF